Issues in Mental Health
Series Editor: Jo Campling

The care and status of persons with mental health problems has been identified as one of the key issues in health and society in the 1990s.

This series of books has been commissioned to give a multi-disciplinary perspective: legal, medical, psychiatric and social work aspects of menta health will be covered. There is also an international perspective: whereve possible, books will compare developments in a range of different countries.

PUBLISHED

Philip Bean and Patricia Mounser
Discharged from Mental Hospitals

Suman Fernando
Mental Health, Race and Culture

Shulamit Ramon (*editor*)
Beyond Community Care: Normalisation and Integration Work

Anne Rogers, David Pilgrim and Ron Lacey
Experiencing Psychiatry: Users' Views of Services

FORTHCOMING

Shulamit Ramon
Mental Health in Europe

The *Issues in Mental Health* series is published in association with:

MIND (National Association for Mental Health)
22 Harley Street, London W1N 2ED (071–637–0741)

MIND is the leading mental health organisation in England and Wales. It works for a better life for people diagnosed, labelled or treated as mentally ill. It does this through campaigning, influencing government policy, training, education and service provision. Throughout its work MIND reflects its awareness of black and ethnic communities, and draws on the expertise of people with direct experience as providers and users of mental health services.

The points of view expressed in this publication do not necessarily reflect MIND policy.

Experiencing Psychiatry

Users' Views of Services

Anne Rogers
David Pilgrim
and
Ron Lacey

MACMILLAN

in association
with

First published 1993 by
MACMILLAN PRESS LTD
Houndmills, Basingstoke, Hampshire RG21 2XS
and London
Companies and representatives
throughout the world

ISBN 0–333–45258–5 hardcover
ISBN 0–333–45259–3 paperback

A catalogue record for this book is available
from the British Library.

11 10 9 8 7 6 5 4 3
03 02 01 00 99 98 97 96 95

Printed in Hong Kong

Series Standing Order   (Issues in Mental Health)

If you would like to receive future titles in this series as they are published, you can make use of our standing order facility. To place a standing order please contact your bookseller or, in case of difficulty, write to us at the address below with your name and address and the name of the series. Please state with which title you wish to begin your standing order. (If you live outside the United Kingdom we may not have the rights for your area, in which case we will forward your order to the publisher concerned.)

Customer Services Department, Macmillan Distribution Ltd
Houndmills, Basingstoke, Hampshire RG21 2XS, England

To all the users who made this book possible

FOOL: ... as a madman's epistles are no gospels, so it matters little when they are delivered.

OLIVIA: How now! art thou mad?

FOOL: No madam, I do but read madness: and your ladyship will have it as it ought to be, you must allow its voice.

Shakespeare, *Twelfth Night*, Act V, Scene 1

Men will always be mad and those who think they can cure them are the maddest of all.

Voltaire, Letter 1762

I have myself spent nine years in a lunatic asylum and have never suffered from the obsession of wanting to kill myself; but I know that each conversation with a psychiatrist in the morning made me want to hang myself because I knew I could not strangle him.

Antonin Artaud, 1896–1948

Contents

List of Figures and Tables

Preface

The survey on which this book is based was undertaken during 1990 by local MIND associations, mental health self-advocacy groups and workers in statutory mental health services. The survey and the analysis of the results were done in collaboration by MIND and Roehampton Institute, London. The questionnaire used examined mental health services in England and Wales through the eyes of people with substantial experience of being at the receiving end of those services. Every one of the 516 people who took part in the research had received at least one period of in-patient treatment in a psychiatric hospital. The questionnaire for the survey was designed on the basis of discussions with psychiatric service users which defined the issues and set the agenda for the survey. This agenda was also shaped by the nature and frequency of enquiries and complaints received by MIND's national and local advice and information services.

The People First survey was a development of a survey amongst chronic tranquilliser users undertaken jointly by MIND and the BBC in 1984. MIND's national and local advice services had been receiving a large volume of enquiries from people experiencing problems with benzodiazepine minor tranquillisers. They complained of side-effects and of difficulties they were experiencing in withdrawing from them. Many people complained that doctors were either ignoring their anxieties about the drugs or dismissing them as symptoms of their problems. A literature search revealed a marked association between the nature of the problems reported to MIND's advice services and reports of adverse effects and the risks of dependence associated with benzodiazepine reported by a substantial body of research. These findings led to MIND launching a sustained public campaign to focus attention on the problems generated by the over-prescription and misuse of benzodiazepine tranquillisers. MIND's special report, *Minor Tranquillisers, Hard Facts – Hard Choices*,[1] launched the campaign and generated widespread media interest in the issues. In 1983 a popular BBC consumer programme reported the stories of three people who said they had become dependent on tranquillisers, which led to more than 3000 letters being received by the programme from people with similar problems. The programme approached MIND with a view to setting up a national telephone counselling service to help people with tranquilliser problems. However, MIND was reluctant to engage in such a massive undertaking and had severe reservations as to the potential value of a telephone counselling approach to the complex problems of so many people. In the light of these reservations it was decided to conduct a survey amongst those who had written to the 'That's Life!' programme. Questionnaires were sent to 3000 viewers and 2150 valid responses were returned. The results of the MIND 'That's Life!' survey were published by BBC Publications in 1985[2] with the expressed intention of putting the experiences of people who had used the drugs into the centre of the public debate. The publicity surrounding minor tranquillisers increased the number of enquiries concerning other types of psychiatric treatment which led to MIND publishing further special reports on other drugs and ECT.[3]

MIND is a 'broad church' which encompasses many varieties and shades of opinion. There are those who subscribe to the medical model of mental illness and its treatment, there are others who are sceptical of the model and an increasingly influential body of users who not only reject the medical model but are vociferously hostile to it. Thus one of the purposes of the People First survey was to reach out to people who had had, or were receiving, mainstream mental health services to inform the sometimes vigorous debates which were taking place within MIND. The major criterion for selecting respondents for the survey was the experience of at least one period of treatment in a psychiatric hospital as an in-patient. We were particularly concerned to seek the views and experiences of people whose needs would be perceived as being at the severe end of the continuum, needs which have traditionally been defined by others, (usually by people with a financial or professional interest in providing mental health services.) The survey was conducted in a climate of rapid change in the location if not the nature of mental health services. Hospitals were closing and people were being discharged into the community. Some patients seem to have rejected whatever services that may have been available to them, whilst others have made the transition with few problems. There has been a great deal of media coverage of the consequences of the inadequate services in the community, and no shortage of people prepared to join in the public debate as to what should be done for the 'mentally ill'. There have been calls to halt mental hospital closures until such time as alternative services become available. However the voices of those for whom mental health services are ostensibly designed have been noticeably absent in the debate. This book represents an attempt to provide a medium through which some of these voices may be heard.

The book is structured in a particular way to try to provide a coherent account of the main findings of the survey. Because of space we have been unable to present every nuance of the data. However, no major finding from the analysis has been omitted. Also we have not only offered the reader a glimpse of these findings in their bald state. They have been put into a context of other work done. For instance at the beginning, even before we get on to our data, we summarise the ways in which existing researchers have dealt with the views of psychiatric patients. Then at the beginning of each chapter, we put the findings into the context of other literature.

After the review of existing work on the patient's view, the ways in which users saw their mental health problem are described and discussed. This is followed by their views of the professionals they encountered. The experience of life both inside and outside of psychiatric facilities is then addressed. Two chapters are then given over to organising our findings on treatment and the respondents' experience of informed consent to that treatment

Finally, we have a concluding chapter which draws out some policy implications of the data as a whole. A methodological appendix is provided in order to provide a full account of the way in which the survey was conducted and our thoughts on the strengths and weaknesses of the sample of patients and ex-patients we accessed.

ANNE ROGERS
DAVID PILGRIM
RON LACEY

References

1. *Minor Tranquillisers: Hard Facts – Hard Choices* (London: MIND, 1982).
2. Lacey, R. and Woodward, S., *That's Life Survey on Tranquillisers* (London: BBC Publications, 1985).
3. *Antidepressants: First Choice or Last Resort?* (1984); *Major Tranquillisers: The Price of Tranquillity* (1985); *Lithium Therapy: Questions of Balance* (1985); *ECT: Pros, Cons and Consequences* (1988).

Acknowledgements

We have already dedicated this book to our most appreciated group of helpers. However thanks are also due to some others. First, whilst we designed and piloted the People First questionnaire, it was disseminated and completed via a variety of local MIND associations and other groups. Thanks to these groups for working so hard and returning the questionnaires by the deadlines set. Second, we are grateful to those students at Roehampton Institute who helped us collate and code the vast mountain of responses generated by our respondents. Third, we would like to express our particular gratitude to Dr Richard Bentall in the Department of Clinical Psychology at Liverpool University for helping us contact pilot respondents and to Dr Graham Fennell at Roehampton Institute for his support during the phase of data analysis.

ANNE ROGERS
DAVID PILGRIM
RON LACEY

1
Views on the Patient's View

Research on the patient's perspective

There has been a growing acceptance over the last few years that health care, like other human services, should be subject to evaluation. It has been suggested this should not only involve measuring medical outcomes, or economic efficiency, but also whether services are socially acceptable.[1] It is this latter aspect, together with the experience of mental health problems, which is the concern of this book. Our central question is this: to what extent are mental health services acceptable to the people who use them? Before going on to address this question in the following chapters, we need to set the scene by putting our study into a wider context of research on the 'patient's view'. Some of this, particularly about psychiatric patients, has reflected professional interests and has failed to take the critical implications of users of services seriously. Let us start by reviewing briefly research on non-psychiatric patients.

Patient satisfaction with health care

Over the last ten years or so, there has been an increasing research interest in the views of patients using general health and hospital services. Studies in this area have revealed some interesting findings and a detailed picture of a patient perspective on health care is gradually being built up. It seems that those using hospital and related services for physical ailments are, on the whole, satisfied with the care they receive,[2] although there is greater scepticism about the beneficial value of prescribed drugs.[3] Also, the increased uptake of alternative therapies may indicate a level of dissatisfaction with more traditional services.[4]

The recent research interest in patient satisfaction appears to have been influenced by changes in the underlying ideology of health care policy. One of the more positive effects of introducing a general management philosophy into the National Health

1

Service (NHS) has been an acknowledgement of the importance of consumer satisfaction. The Griffiths Report (*Community Care: Agenda for Action*),[5] for example, emphasised the importance of the health service being accountable to patients. The importance of consumer choice has also been stressed in recent government consultative documents on primary care, and it was central to widespread changes envisaged by the 1989 White Paper, *Patients First*, now made law in the 1990 NHS and Community Care Act. However, this acknowledgement of the rights of health service users has yet to be translated into a full commitment to user participation. As it stands, present policy is rhetorically about consumers but actually it is about the purchasers of services: that is, health authorities. The latter need only incorporate a consumer perspective when, and if, it is expedient.

Professionals also seem to have been increasingly interested in user's views, albeit usually from a paternalistic position. The goal of compliance with treatments prescribed by medical practitioners, accompanied by an uncritical acceptance of the inherent desirability of professional practices, often seem to lurk behind a concern to find out the 'patient's views'. For example, in a classic study by Helman,[6] doctors wanted to know more about how people viewed their illnesses. This was linked to a concern to refute the legitimacy of folk remedies and to reduce 'non-compliance' with the prescribed treatments of official medicine.

Psychiatric services

Whatever the shortcomings of approaches to evaluating health care for those using the health service for physical complaints, there is now a clear acceptance within health policy circles that more credence and authority should be given to the patient's perspective. The same cannot be said for the views of psychiatric patients. Although, belatedly, there have been signs that the views of users of mental health services should be taken on board more than hitherto, this has not been as widely accepted or uncontentious as, say, seeking the views of patients visiting their General Practitioner (GP) for minor ailments. Yet there are a number of important reasons why mental health users have as much, if not more, of a valid claim to having their views taken seriously as other groups of patients.

First, attention given to psychiatric patients' views and levels of satisfaction with services has lagged behind that given to other client groups using health service facilities. This is largely a result of the widely held view that psychiatric patients are automatically incapable of providing a rational or valid opinion about the services they are using. (The way in which mental patients' views have been portrayed is examined in more detail below.) This view also seems to be shared by those who have the main responsibility for financing research into mental health. They seem not to be seriously concerned with what the users of services and the subjects of medical treatments have to say about what is being produced, supposedly on their behalf. For example, if one looks at the Medical Research Council's priorities for the funding of research into 'schizophrenia', then the users' perspective is nowhere to be seen.[7] Despite the failure of over 90 years of research into 'schizophrenia' to discover a specific aetiology, of the ten recommendations regarding future research, top of the list comes 'genetic investigations', followed by 'neuropathological studies of post-mortem brains'. Evaluation of services *to* patients is number 8 out of the 10 priorities, and *user* evaluation of services and treatment is not mentioned at all.

Second, contact with services for those with mental health problems is far more extensive than for most others who use the health and social services (although they have this in common with some groups of physically disabled people). Those who enter hospital for acute physical problems, such as appendicitis, are patients for a short time only, whether or not they experience their hospitalisation as positive or negative; thus the quality of service and treatment does not have as many long-term consequences as for those who are psychiatric patients. The latter often spend many years of their lives in contact with services and professionals.

Third, the consequences of being labelled 'ill' are often greater for a person who is given a psychiatric diagnosis. For the majority of those with physical problems, the diagnosis itself is often only a temporary one and is often not stigmatising. In contrast, a psychiatric label is often for life. No matter how hard psychiatrists have tried to equate psychiatric diagnoses with those of physical illness, the notion of mental illness is still peculiarly stigmatising. This equation is also fundamentally flawed, as was pointed out some time ago by Wooton.[8] Since the diagnosis of a person as 'mentally ill' is done primarily on the basis of a judgement about a person's conduct, there is always a risk of invalidating their whole identity or sense of self.

Over and above the potential damage that a label of mental illness can have subjectively on the 'self', the social and economic consequences of contact with psychiatric services (as confirmed by this study) are objectively enormous. Those labelled as mentally ill are discriminated against by present and prospective employers, and are often subjected to a life of poverty as a result. Educational opportunities are curtailed, family and intimate relationships are affected and making social contact with people is fraught with difficulties.

Given the vast array of negative effects associated with becoming a psychiatric patient, it seems a minimum requirement on the part of service providers and policy-makers that efforts are made to ascertain and comply with patients' views and experiences of services. After all, mental health professionals are responsible for providing services that are ostensibly designed to meet their patients' needs. It is also incumbent on service providers, as it is with any other group in society who are in a powerful position, to be accountable for the practices they adopt and the services they deliver.

The mental health users' movement: demanding change

The absence of accountability of service providers, together with a growing dissatisfaction with contemporary responses to people suffering from mental distress, gave rise to a vibrant and growing mental health users' movement during the 1980s. This movement has been busy campaigning for the civil rights of psychiatric patients and alternatives to present treatment regimes. Three examples give a flavour of the type of activism which has emerged in the area of user participation and mental health services. In 1988, a campaign was launched by users in London to oppose changes being advocated by the Royal College of Psychiatrists to the 1983 Mental Health Act. The proposed Community Treatment Order (CTOs) would have allowed doctors to treat patients in the community on a compulsory basis. This hostility to CTOs culminated in over 100 users and their allies marching from Hyde Park to Belgrave Square. There, a wreath was laid at the steps of the Royal College of Psychiatrists, in honour of the deceased recipients of electro-convulsive therapy (ECT) and major tranquillisers. Speeches were made (including one from a Labour MP) and patients read poems critical of psychiatric treatment.

A second example of the activity during this period was that of organised opposition to a poster campaign in the south of England by SANE (Schizophrenia — A National Emergency). This advertising campaign enjoyed the patronage of Prince Charles and the pop singer, 'Sting'. It was heavily financed by, amongst others, Rupert Murdoch and P&O ferries. The posters depicted psychiatric patients as frenziedly dangerous and called for a halt to the present hospital closure programme. In response, London-based users' groups lobbied the Advertising Standards Authority about the offending posters.

A third example was the lobby of the Opposition spokespeople in Parliament by a national network of 56 different users' groups. This network is dispersed throughout the country. The MPs agreed to meet the groups, to hear their complaints about existing services and their recommendations for changes in mental health policy.

Thus, user dissatisfaction has reached such a point that, in terms of numbers and organisations, it now constitutes a nascent 'new social movement'.[9] The rise of the mental health users' movement suggests that there is a groundswell of dissatisfaction which health and social services have, overall, failed to contain. There are, of course, exceptions: for example, receptive managers were crucial to the funding and development of the Nottingham Patients Council (a hospital-based user-run advocacy scheme which meets regularly with representatives of the hospital management). However, such examples stand in isolation as models of good practice, which as yet have not been emulated elsewhere.

Taking our lead from the concerns expressed by this growing users' movement, the aim of the survey reported here is, we hope, a further step towards pressing for more accountable services based on a comprehensive picture of users' views and requirements. Before going on to outline the particular 'patient' perspective we adopt in the rest of the book, it is useful to set this against a backdrop of how psychiatric patients' views have previously been portrayed.

The portrayal of psychiatric patients in research

More often than not psychiatric patients' views are simply excluded from health service 'satisfaction' research[10] or, for that matter, research on other subjects. Even sociologists who are careful to include the views of other marginalised groups in society, and who question taken-for-granted-assumptions, seem to accept implicitly that psychiatric patients' views are, by definition, invalid.

With regard to the more specific area of psychiatry and mental health services, patients' views are hardly referred to at all. Mental patients are frequently only seen as the passive objects of study, whose individual characteristics and feelings are mostly variables to be 'controlled out' in order to ensure valid results. In this, psychiatry is no different from other scientific and medical research in which experimental design can play an important role in the evaluation of medical procedures and therapies. However, we question whether such an approach to research actually serves the long-term interests of patients. It has certainly not encouraged therapeutic alternatives to date which are acceptable to service users.

Where there is some mention of psychiatric patients' views, explicitly or implicitly, 'mental patients' are portrayed in a pejorative light. Basically, the views of those diagnosed as mentally ill, especially those who are critical or unappreciative of contemporary mental health services, are not to be trusted. A review of the literature provides a number of interesting versions of this claim. Here we mention four types.

1. The disregarding of users' views which do not coincide with those of mental health professionals by researchers

In an early attempt at providing a genuine user perspective, Mills found some interesting results.[11] The study, which used mainly the accounts of patients and their relatives, found that users of services preferred contact with non-professionals to contact with social and health services personnel. When the latter were 'from a different social class [they] were often received with hostility'. The greatest forms of support were regarded as coming from people such as the local publican, the secretary of the local darts club and home helps, who were seen to provide 'down to earth common sense'. However, a reviewer of this work (Kathleen Jones, now Professor of Social Policy at York) appeared to dismiss this errant view of services:

> It is hard to believe that there were no sympathetic and sensible social workers in the area ... The material is taken very largely from patients and their relatives and no attempt at validation appears to have been

made. Since some of the patients were suffering from paranoia, and others from depression, it would have been a basic precaution to check the objective value of statements with the medical records or the responsible psychiatrist.[12] (p. 343)

Cross-validation, using multiple methods, is certainly a principle to be honoured in research. However, if one is going to advocate this position, surely it should apply to all psychiatric research and professionals, and not just studies that attempt to take users views seriously. Yet it is striking that there are few demands from eminent professors to validate the views of psychiatrists or social workers against those of their clients. Arguably, professionals are as (if not more) likely to adopt a distorted view of patients and their own practices because of their socialisation. This leads professionals to assume that 'their' view is by and large superior to those of patients and relatives and that their practices are unquestionably useful.

The notion that statements from professionals (or any other quarter) can have an uncomplicated 'objective value' is to us highly dubious. All that we can say for certain is that different groups express their views in the light of their experience and with due consideration to their interests. Professionals and clients have their own experiences and interests which shape their accounts of reality. This is not to argue that there may not be objective indicators which might resolve differences of opinion between these groups (such as the manifest effects of being given tranquillisers). Even here, as we will show later, what professionals deem to be salient aspects of reality may not be the same as those which recipients would pick out.

2. The continued prevalence of the notion that psychiatric patients are continually irrational and so incapable of giving a valid view

Discussions around informed consent (consent based on adequate and understandable information) which are relevant to the administration of treatments and participation in research programmes is another area where users' views are often invalidated. 'Schizophrenics' are a particular group thought inherently incapable of giving *genuine* informed consent. This is not infrequently linked to the high rate of 'non-compliance' to prescribed medication: 'Since the majority of clients with schizophrenia deny their illness, special difficulties are encountered in the criteria for understanding the nature of the psychiatric condition...Denial is a major psychopathological mechanism which can impair appreciation' (p. 385).[13]

Why those labelled as schizophrenic should be so eager to 'deny' their 'illness' is left unexplored. We are simply provided with the traditional assumption of lack of 'insight', this being defined, in a circular fashion, as existing when you agree with the opinion of your treating psychiatrist. The diagnostic label of 'schizophrenia' is taken as a neutral one that can only be of benefit to patients. The question of the stigmatising effects of labelling by professionals are not generally considered. As one user poignantly put it recently, a label of mental illness had not exactly helped him 'on the dance floors of life'. Similarly, there is little concern with ascertaining the reasons for the high rate of 'non-compliance' with a medical regimen. The iatrogenic effects of such medication (described in Chapter 6) suggests that there are very good rational reasons why such high rates of non-compliance with medication occur.

Assumptions about the inability of patients to hold valid opinions are held by therapists of all kinds. This view is summarised in a literature review of consumer satisfaction with mental health treatment by Lebow,[14] who notes that therapists of all types often suggest that the consumer cannot adequately judge the treatments they are given:

> Distortion is seen as inherent in consumer evaluation because of the client's intensity of involvement in treatment and impaired mental status, and the client is viewed as lacking the requisite experience to assess treatment adequately. Consumer satisfaction is regarded as principally determined by transference projections, cognitive dissonance, unconscious processes, folie a deux, client character, and a naivety about treatment, rather than an informed decision process reflecting the adequacy of treatment. (p. 254)

Often there are more explicit prejudicial views held of psychiatric patients by health professionals. The second biennial report of the Mental Health Act Commission noted the worrying tendency of staff to dismiss complaints made by patients as being simply part of their psychopathology.[15] Negative views extend to staff in accident and emergency departments, where psychiatric patients may be classified as 'rubbish' compared to the 'real' work of casualty staff.[16] This is, of course, not a very comforting thought for users when there is push to concentrate acute psychiatric services on District General Hospital (DGH) sites. The first port of call in a crisis commonly might be the casualty department.

3. *Patients and relatives are assumed to share the same interests and, where they do not, the views of the former are disregarded by researchers*

Another tendency in work that ostensibly sets out to give credence to the consumer's view is the conflation of the patient's view with that of their relatives. This is evident in a study which set out to examine the impact of the 1959 Mental Health Act.[17] The authors of the study conclude that: 'On the whole, the general picture given here is of a large degree of satisfaction on the part of patients and their relatives' (p. 130).

However, if one scrutinises their results in detail, there are some important discrepancies found between relatives' and patients' views. Whereas 84 per cent of the relatives' group were favourably disposed to the admission of the patient, only 47 per cent of the patients were content to be admitted, with 43 per cent being reluctant. Yet the implications of these findings, which seem to suggest on close reading that the interests of these two groups may at times be divergent, was not noted by the researchers. Moreover, disquieting results were glossed over and excused by referring to patient pathology. For instance, complaints made by patients about services were dismissed thus: 'Their complaints referred to rough handling by nursing staff. It must be remembered that they were rather sick patients, and it was also not within our brief to verify individual complaints' (p. 126).

As we will see later, accounts of brutal treatment by staff from patients remain today. One might be inclined to dismiss this example, taken from the 1960s, as the result of the paternalism of the past. However, more up-to-date examples, as discussed previously, suggest that there is no automatic acceptance of patients' own attribution of meanings, or indeed their rights to ordinary civil liberties, such as genuine consent to treatment.

4. *Giving partial credence to the client's perspective provided that it fits in with the expert's view*

Often lay conceptions of mental health problems are researched in such a way that there is little room for people to express their own view about the subject in hand. One recent example, from a psychologist's perspective,[18] involved a research design aimed at examining lay people's conceptions of 'neuroticism'. Leaving aside the problem of representativeness (the experimental group was 'a fairly homogeneous young, well-educated sample'), such questionnaires leave little room for self-expression since all the items are predetermined as standardised items by the researcher, with no open-ended questions.

Even where credence is ostensibly given to the freely expressed views of patients, there is a tendency on the part of some researchers (who are usually also mental health practitioners) to adopt a 'victim blaming' approach. This approach tends to leave the practitioners' own role and that of their service unquestioned. One example of this is a study which found that clients attending a psychiatric day unit found it stigmatising.[19] Patients preferred to 'hide' the reasons for attendance, because a label of 'mental illness' was experienced to be unhelpful. The analysis focused on the need for clients to be helped 'to arrive at unambiguous personal interpretations and management of the stigmatising reaction of the local community' (p. 345). It is suggested that 'if they [the patients] are supported in their attempts to understand and manage the resulting stigma, then the social and therapeutic effectiveness of the service should increase'. The professionals' role in alleviating stigma was outlined as the 'need to encourage clients to be open about their fears, and to help them demystify the idea of psychiatric care'. Why users should be given the onerous task of promoting and legitimising a stigmatising service is not explained. A more pertinent question, which was not considered, is why it was seen as acceptable, in principle, to go on offering a service that users found stigmatising and unhelpful. Clearly the researcher's own professional interests would have then been at stake.

A more recent example is that of a study reported in the *British Medical Journal*,[20] the aim of which was to obtain the views of psychiatric in-patients. The most important finding of the study appeared to be that the 'thing psychiatric inpatients value most about being in hospital is their ability to leave'. The use of drugs was not rated highly and 'talking' to a care giver was seen as the most valuable aspect of being an in-patient. The authors conclude that 'talking therapy' should be given a higher priority during psychiatric training. However, the authors did not take the customers' view about leaving hospital to its logical conclusion. If they had, they would have had to question the value, in principle, of becoming an in-patient in a DGH psychiatric unit. The customers' view might well be important to the researchers, but the equally important notion that 'the customer is always right' is not conceded. Where there is a fundamental questioning of the value of hospital admission, which may well lead to a questioning of the inherent value of existing services, and all the professional interest this implies, the patients' view is evaded. Ignorance, like knowledge, can be goal-directed.

There is a small amount of research which does not presume that mental health services are only there to do people good. An early example of this was the work of Mayer and Timms[21] in which social workers were encouraged to heed seriously the views expressed by clients. More recently Bean, in a small sample study, showed that the reasons patients gave for being in hospital differed markedly from the assumptions of the professionals.[22] Patients thought they were in hospital for 'a rest', whilst practitioners tended to view their stay in legalistic terms, according to their status as detained or voluntary patients. The work of Beresford and Croft[23] also highlights the views of users of social services and emphasises the need for genuine participation by users in research about services. More recently, Barham and Hayward[24] have made use of qualitative interviews with ex-mental patients to explore their experiences of trying to live outside hospital.

Two other examples indicate an acceptance of the users' perspective as it is *actually* expressed. The Community Psychiatric Nurses' Association produced a booklet in which verbatim quotation were recorded from patients discharged from hospital on a range of issues affecting their lives.[25] These included stigma, finances, 'what's needed in hospital', living alone and moving out of hospital, attitudes towards services, treatments and accommodation and ways of coping. Similarly, a publication produced by Islington Mental Health Forum[26] examines a group of users' views regarding the effects of diagnosis and medication, and suggestions about alternatives. Both these publications, based on gathering information from local groups of patients, are a marked departure from the dominant way in which psychiatric patients' views are depicted by researchers.

The aim of reporting the outcome of the People First survey in this book is to extend this type of analysis in a more systematic way. We will encompass a larger number of responses from users of psychiatric services than these small-scale studies.

From research on users to research for and by users

Many of the authors of the studies discussed above show a genuine interest in the views of clients. However, two further aspects seem vital to ensuring a genuine reflection of users' views. First, there needs to be a questioning of the assumptions of the researcher and those of the discipline and profession from which they come. Whether it is psychology, psychiatry, social work, sociology or nursing, claims of taking the consumer seriously must be followed through with reference to the meaning that users themselves give to their experiences and the implications that follow from this. For instance, if the thing users like best about hospital is their opportunity to leave this suggests the need for researchers fundamentally to question the value of continuing this form of service.

Second, there needs to be more of an attempt to involve users themselves in research. Health and social services concerned with evaluation research need to take into account a user perspective, perhaps by employing researchers who have been on the receiving end of psychiatry to do field work. Increasing access to higher education for those who have previously missed out on educational opportunity through mental distress or being in the psychiatric system is another consideration. The effect of such policy changes would take time. However, given that *all* mental health services have access to clients, there is no reason why a user perspective could not be built into all mental health research, whether it seeks to find 'the causes' of mental health problems or is concerned with treatment, rehabilitation or the implementation of community care policies. In short, it is time to move away from research on users to research for and by users.

The People First survey involved users in three main ways, other than as respondents of the lengthy interviews used. First, in order to gain access to a suitable sample, users in MIND groups up and down the country were crucial in making the right contacts. Second, users were heavily involved as data collectors. Many users and ex-users interviewed fellow-users. Third, in the dissemination of findings, a steering group was set up by National MIND to co-ordinate campaigns which used the People First material. User representatives were involved in this group, and users in MIND were invited to participate actively in the design and execution of six campaigns flowing from the survey data. Nonetheless, we recognise that this is only a step towards user involvement in the research process. Users should, for example, be consulted about the topics that are included in the interview and the data analysis. Since the analysis and interpretation of the data has been carried out, by and large, by the authors alone, it is important for us to outline both our value standpoint and the conceptual framework used to analyse the data.

In terms of the motivation for carrying out a study of this type, we distance ourselves from those who think that patients' views are important to ensure greater compliance with 'treatment'. Though there may well be genuine worries regarding the continuing uptake of services, when the old Victorian asylums eventually do close we do not think that a professional or bio-medical definition of services should set the benchmark against which patients' views should be evaluated; thus whether people use services in a way the professionals would like to see them used is not the primary focus here.

Our approach starts from the premise that the views of users of mental health services are valid in their own right. We do not assume that these views are a definitive version of reality or 'the truth', but they are a legitimate version of reality, or a truth, which professionals and policy-makers should no longer evade or dismiss. We assume that people think about and explain the causes and experience of their mental health problems, use of services and treatments in their own way, and that this is worthy of documentation. The views may, quite legitimately, be very different from those of professionals. The latter have disseminated their views as expert knowledge. Targets of that knowledge have had few opportunities to comment. This book gives them such a chance.

The patients' view is particularly relevant today. The contemporary debates about community care are only meaningful if they take into consideration not only *where* services are geographically situated, but also the content and nature of the service on offer. The accountability and the shape and content of services is a matter as much (if not more) for the users of services to pass judgement on, as it is for the managers and professionals gaining a livelihood from running such services.

There has been much criticism of 'satisfaction' research using only fixed-choice questions. Such survey research presents a picture of patients as fixed objects devoid of any values. We attempt to avoid this here. Fixed-choice rating scales are used to give an overall assessment of whether aspects of services are viewed as satisfactory or not. These provide a gross but important indicator of the extent to which the users in the survey viewed the service or treatment overall. Thus the presentation of this more quantitative data is designed to give a summary picture of the respondents' evaluations. This is supplemented by users' own words in response to open-ended questions.

The purpose of using this more qualitative data is twofold. First, it is designed to build up a comprehensive picture of the particular aspects of treatment or services under consideration by presenting examples of the whole range of views expressed in detail. Second, it aims to illuminate those finer details of the subjective experience of users that are obscured by, or submerged in, the more quantitative data.[27] More will be said about the data and its utility in the next chapter and in the methodological appendix we supply at the end of the book.

Wherever possible in the text, we have tried to give a feel of the content and range of views expressed by users of the relevant issues. The nature of these views differs according to the topic under investigation. In the first part of the book, the focus is on *users' conceptions* of mental health problems and how these differ from professionals. *Users' experience* in relation to hospitalisation and treatment, and views of how patients are dealt with by different mental health professionals, is referred to throughout. This is closely linked to, and overlaps with, *users' satisfaction*: that is, how satisfied were the respondents of this survey with the treatments and services they have received. This question of satisfaction becomes particularly important later in the book when we address the issue of how patients evaluate the treatments they have received. Judgements about outcomes are determined also by expectations, so that linked closely to this concept is that of *users' expectations*. Satisfaction with services only makes sense in terms of the aspirations and expectations that users have about the services and professionals they use.

The implications of these different users' views are also integral to this book. Expectations may be so fundamentally at odds with what is on offer that tinkering with the professional–client relationship (through increased 'communication', for example) may be a doomed solution. By paying attention to the users' collective voice through a close reading of the data, we have tried to present policy implications which follow on from the majority views in the survey. We hope that those responsible for services will give due consideration to what is being said by those for whom such services are supposedly run.

References

1. Doll, R., 'Monitoring the National Health Service', *Proceedings of the Royal Society of Medicine*, 66 (1973), pp. 729–40
2. Locker, D. and Dunt, D., 'Theoretical and Methodological Issues in Sociological Studies of Consumer Satisfaction with Medical Care', *Social Science and Medicine*, 12, 4 (1978), pp. 283–92.
3. Calnan, M., 'Lay Evaluation of Medicine and Medical Practice: Report of a Pilot Study', *International Journal of Health Services*, 18, 2 (1988), pp. 311–23.
4. Sharma, U., 'Using Alternative Therapies' Abbott, P. and Payne, G. (eds), in *New Directions in the Sociology of Health*, (Lander: Falmer Press, 1990).
5. London: Her Majesty's Stationary Office (HMSO), 1990.
6. Helman, C., ' "Feed a Cold, Starve a Fever" – Folk Models of Infection in an English Suburban Community', *Culture, Medicine and Psychiatry*, 2, 2 (1978), pp. 107–37.
7. Medical Research Council, *Research into Schizophrenia: Report of the Schizophrenia and Allied Conditions Committee to the Neurosciences Board* (London, 1988).
8. Wooton, B., *Social Science and Social Pathology* (London: George Allen & Unwin, 1959).
9. Rogers, A. and Pilgrim, D., 'Pulling Down Churches: Accounting for the British Mental Health User's Movement', *Sociology of Health and Illness*, 13, 2 (June 1991), pp. 129–48.
10. See, for example, Hall, J. and Dornan, M., 'What Patients Like about their Medical Care and How Often they are asked: A Meta-Analysis of the Satisfaction Literature, *Social Science and Medicine*, 27, 9 (1988) pp. 935–9.
11. Mills, E., *Living with Mental Illness* (London: Institute of Community Studies/Routledge & Kegan Paul, 1962).
12. Jones, K., book review in *Sociological Review*, 8 (1962), pp. 343–4.
13. Davidhazar, D., and Wehlage, D., 'Can the Client with Chronic Schizophrenia Consent to Nursing Research?' *Journal of Advanced Nursing*, 9 (1984), pp. 381–90.
14. Lebow, J., 'Consumer Satisfaction with Mental Health Treatment', *Psychological Bulletin*, 91, 2 (1982), pp. 244–59.
15. Mental Health Act Commission, London, *2nd Biennial Report* (1988).
16. Jeffrey, R., 'Normal Rubbish: Deviant Patients in Casualty Departments', *Sociology of Health and Illness*, 1 (1979), pp. 90–107.
17. Hoenig, J. and Hamilton, M., *The Desegregation of the Mentally Ill* (London: Routledge & Kegan Paul, 1969).
18. Furnham, A., 'Lay Conceptions of Neuroticism', *Personal and Individual Difference*, 5, 1 (1984), pp. 95–103
19. Teasdale, K., 'Stigma and Psychiatric Day Care', *Journal of Advanced Nursing*, 12 (1987), pp. 339–46.
20. McIntyre, K., Farrell, M. and David, A., 'What do Psychiatric Inpatients Really Want?' *British Medical Journal*, 298 (21 January 1989), pp. 159–60.
21. Mayer, J. and Timms, N., *The Client Speaks* (London: Routledge & Kegan Paul, 1970).
22. Bean, P., *Compulsory Admissions to Mental Hospitals* (Chichester: Wiley, 1980).

23. Beresford, P. and Croft, S., *Whose Welfare?: Private Care or Public Service* (Brighton: Lewis Cohen Urban Studies, 1986).
24. Barham, P. and Hayward, R., *From the Mental Patient to the Person* (London: Routledge and Kegan Paul, 1991).
25. Community Psychiatric Nurses' Association, *The Patient's Case* (London, 1989).
26. Islington Mental Health Forum, *Fit for Consumption? Mental Health Users' Views of Treatment in Islington* (London, 1989).
27. A more detailed methodological account of the research is provided in the methodological appendix.

2
Early Experiences of Mental Health Problems

In recent years, a controversy has raged about the nature of distressed or distressing conduct. On the one hand, most psychiatrists argue that they are simply a version of illness. In opposition, a minority of their colleagues have argued that mental illness is a 'myth' as it has no proven biological cause. Instead, it is claimed that psychiatric patients are not ill but that they have 'problems of living'. The latter are about difficulties in how to live one's life. Consequently, what is called mental illness is actually a dustbin label for a variety of moral and existential questions about norms of conduct and the violations of these norms. This view, championed by the American psychoanalyst, Thomas Szasz,[1] depicts psychiatrists as agents of social control hired by the state to smooth over the crises precipitated by the actions of disruptive 'patients' in the presence of their intolerant fellow citizens.

Both these perspectives, in different ways, argue for a privileged view of mental health by experts. The first (and dominant) group insists that the illness conception in accurate and that the public and politicians should leave the understanding and management of 'mental illness' to doctors. The second argues that the personal difficulties experienced by people with the label of mental illness can be best understood by psychotherapists adopting a version of psychoanalysis, existentialism or family systems theory.[2] They emphasise that the 'symptoms' of mental illness are meaningful, rather than pathological and invalid, but that this meaning can only be made understandable via voluntary co-operative relationships between clients and their therapists. Thus some form of psychotherapeutic expertise is deemed to be necessary before those suffering mental distress can figure out the meaning of their experience.

A third position, which is taken by the authors here, is that both physical and mental illnesses are socially negotiated, and those deemed to be suffering from them on a short-term ('acute') or long-term ('chronic') basis have something of value to say directly from their experience. Moreover, as will be seen, the issue of *power* over how a problem is understood, and by whom, is central to any understanding of what happens when a person has early contact with mental health professionals. As Scott[4] has pointed out, a psychiatric crisis and its resolution entail a negotiation between three different parties: professionals (GPs, social workers, the police, psychiatrists); prospective patients; and those connected to them in their immediate social network (relatives, friends, neighbours or even strangers).

Whereas textbooks written for and by professionals describe mental abnormality and distress, as was seen in the last chapter it is rare for the patient's perspective to be given much credence. This is clearly a gross oversight which we hope to correct in this book. As Scott (himself, like Szasz, a psychoanalyst and psychiatrist) notes, patients are one of the three key sets of actors involved in the negotiation of the social reality of mental illness in contemporary society. This being the case, we need to hear from them, and not just from their relatives or the professionals they encounter.

Coulter[5] notes that the early negotiation about what constitutes mental disorder occurs first in the 'lay' area of the street or the domestic setting, before professionals are contacted. The latter then arrive on the scene, once this initial labelling has taken place, to 'rubber stamp' decisions made already. For example, an unemployed young man living at home with his parents locks himself in his room and refuses to eat for several days, claiming that they are trying to poison his food. They ring the GP. The doctor cannot coax the man out of his room   and suggests that he may be entering a schizophrenic illness. Later, a psychiatrist and social worker arrive and force the man to go to hospital under a section of the Mental Health Act. He screams during the drama that his parents, not he, should be locked up.

Or, in another example, a middle-aged woman stands outside a shop and distresses customers by alternatively crying and being abusive, in ways which do not make sense. The shopkeeper, fearful of his trade being affected, and perplexed himself by the commotion, rings the police. They arrive within minutes. They take the woman away under a section of the Mental Health Act for assessment by a psychiatrist.

These are one version of negotiation, where those in the lay network of the incipient patient use their power to bring to an end distress or disruption in their lives. In both examples the patient has little obvious say in the matter about their involuntary removal from civil society as it is the actions of others which decide the outcome. It is important to note that, in the build-up to the crisis, the patient-to-be may have, with varying degrees of awareness, acted to initiate the drama. However, if a plea for help was entailed, at least in these examples, the communication was being made in an indirect or even obscure way. They were not simply saying to the outside world, 'I need help, please'.

In another version, powers of negotiation may be different. A woman meets a friend for a drink whom she has not seen for a while. The friend notices during the evening that the woman is drinking well in excess of her normal amount. They begin to talk and the woman confesses that, since the recent break-up of a sexual relationship, she has been depressed and has thought about ending her life. The friend persuades the woman to seek professional help, and stays with her that night and goes with her to the doctor the following day. The doctor assures the woman that it would be in her interest if he were to arrange for her to be admitted, voluntarily, to the local psychiatric unit. She accepts the advice and her friend drives her to the hospital, where she stays for a few weeks and is given anti-depressants. In this example, the voluntary nature of the admission distinguishes it from the previous cases. Notice still, though, how informal powers (of persuasion) have been influential in the outcome.

In both coercive and voluntary early contact with mental health services, several social processes are in operation with a number of ambiguous emotional consequences. The patient-to-be may or may not be acting in a way which others can understand. These others may or may not themselves become disturbed by what is happening. If they are disturbed, their own feelings of distress may prompt the request for professional intervention. To various degrees the actions of the patient-to-be will be disruptive to orderly existence in public or in private. The more disruptive it is, the more others may be motivated to co-operate with the forced loss of liberty without trial for a relative or fellow citizen.

In the traditional medical view, these hidden social processes of negotiation about what is a problem and what should be done by whom and to whom are rarely acknowledged as important.

Instead, psychiatrists would probably think in terms of cases of mental illness being brought to their attention for diagnosis and treatment. By contrast, those following Szasz and Laing, and sensitive to these social processes, would want to distinguish between coerced and voluntary therapeutic relationships, and would suggest that eventually the behaviour of the patient could be rendered intelligible given enough time and interpretive skill on the part of the therapists. Our view is that this may be achievable but not necessarily; the meaning of distressed and distressing behaviour may remain permanently elusive. What is important, though, it that in the midst of the early part of a drama, where one person takes on (or is designated by others to play) the role of a psychiatric patient, their view of the situation is documented.

Of course, the Szaszians and Laingians might say that their case studies have already provided such a documentation, which can be added to the studies of the 'degradation rituals' performed on patients entering psychiatric hospitals. For instance, Erving Goffman[6] describes ways in which patients entering hospital are systematically stripped of their identity. Whilst this 'patient-centred' attempt to reveal the plight of patients at the mercy of a psychiatric system has been illuminating, it is still the view packaged and interpreted by sympathetic experts. By the 1980s these critics from the 1960s had won the battle of convincing most professionals that large Victorian hospitals were degrading and anti-therapeutic (although a minority of reactionary psychiatrists and their allies are still arguing for their retention). What the critics did not do was persuade the majority that traditional forms of treatment and diagnosis should also be consigned to history. At present the signs are that most psychiatrists are intent on exporting these traditions from the 'bin' to the community.

These efforts on the part of humanistic critics of traditional psychiatry tend to emphasise ways in which the plight of particular *individuals* might be responded to and understood. What is missing from their contribution is any wider documentation of the patient's perspective on their early 'careers'. Goffman was essentially using the fate of individuals to make a moral point about the degradation of total institutions. Our interest is in finding out, from patients' accounts, what they think of their problems and how others react to them. We believe that the data to be presented from the People First survey begins to offer such a collective voice from psychiatric patients. What will be presented in this chapter will be the views of patients responding to those Patients First questions which addressed their view of the early circumstances surrounding the development of their problem and the early experience of mental health professionals.

We are still a third party summarising and editing these views for the reader's attention but we hope we are, as much as possible, letting the patients speak for themselves by drawing on two types of information taken from the survey. First, using the information provided by the 516 respondents, we can give a *quantitative* picture of a number of issues. For instance, this can tell us how may people thought that their problems were bound up with, say, bereavement or loss. Second, by selecting out cases who answered open-ended questions, a *qualitative* view can be built up of the patients' perspective. For instance, in this chapter we will examine responses to questions such as, 'If your first experience of these problems did have an effect on your life can you briefly explain in what ways?'

By blending information of this quantitative and qualitative type, the survey has provided us with a rich picture of the way the respondents answering the questionnaire experienced various aspects of their lives. It also has the advantage of offering information to the reader which is derived from a large group of patients (so it cannot be dismissed as idiosyncratic), whilst providing examples of individual responses (so it cannot be dismissed as just a set of statistics). In this way, overall trends of opinion will be investigated, as well as the finer grain of people's experiences. (At the back of the book is a longer methodological account of the survey if the reader is interested.)

Presentation of findings

For those unfamiliar with the presentation of survey data, a brief explanation will be given about the conventions to be used in this and subsequent chapters. As was noted above, the information provided will be in both quantitative and qualitative form. The former may be offered in a table for convenience. At other times, when there is less information to communicate, this information may simply be presented as part of a statement. Although the total sample in the survey was 516, not all of these people answered all questions. For this reason, when the tables are presented the actual numbers involved will be recorded precisely using the letter *N* (for example, *N* = 423). Also note that is some tables, where only one answer per respondent was used, the total will equal 100 per cent (see Table 2.1). On other occasions the percentages may add up to more than 100 because each subject may have given more than one answer (see Table 2.2), or to nearly 100 in the case of figures being rounded up or down.

The first question that was asked of the respondents in the survey related to what they saw as the reasons for their first contact with the mental health services (see Table 2.1). Given that these were all retrospective accounts of people who had had at least one in-patient stay, remarkably few described this early contact as being because of 'mental illness'. Of those answering this question, only 10.7 per cent considered this to be the reason for contact with services. Given that most of them would have been labelled by psychiatrists as having suffered from some form of mental illness, this indicates at the outset that a substantial discrepancy seems to exist in the basic way in which professionals and users of services construe the fundamental problem. It is worth noting in this regard that the sub-group of patients which did prefer the illness label showed a greater tendency to view services more positively than fellow-patients who eschewed an illness description. This seems to fit the common-sense assumption that, if experts and their clients agree with one another, the latter will be more likely to place a positive value on their experience.

Table 2.1   Reasons for first contact with mental health services

Reason given for contact	%
Mental illness	10.7
Marital problems	10.1
Work stress	9.3
Bereavement/loss	7.9
Physical illness	5.5
Study stress	4.5
Drugs	3.6
Problems with friends/neighbours	2.8
Unemployment	2.0
Sexual identity	1.2
Financial difficulties	0.6
Other	41.8

N = 507

As can be seen from Table 2.1, a wide range of reasons for contact were given by the respondents, including a very large 'other' category (41.8 per cent). This last category seems to suggest that people with problems are likely to understand them or their development in very varied or even idiosyncratic ways, bound up with the particular personal circumstances of the individual.

The sample of people studied suggests that first contact with services typically occurs during young adulthood, with over 80 per cent having contact before the age of 34 and 54 per cent before the age of 24. This may indicate that the challenges of transition from adolescence to adulthood (about employment, identity, education, and so on) may be vital factors in understanding the reasons or the triggers for the initial development of mental health problems. Once the problems developed, the lives of the respondents were affected in a number of ways. Table 2.2 gives a sense of this range of effects.

Table 2.2   Aspects of life affected by mental health problems

Aspects of life affected	%
Self-confidence	82.0
Family relationships	73.6
Hopes for future	71.3
Job	61.6
Relations with friends	59.3
Financial situation	58.3
Education	34.9
Other	24.2

$N = 516$

As can be seen, intimate relationships are notably affected by mental health problems, as are career prospects. The largest adverse effect is simply on the person's self-confidence. Of course, it may be difficult to disentangle cause and effect here: a poor sense of self-confidence and difficulties in relationships and career also *precede* problems developing, as responses to other questions show. The respondents were then asked to expand, in their own terms, on how the above areas of their lives were affected.

Concerning the impact on how people saw their future, this was overwhelmingly negative. Typical responses were: 'I could see no future'; 'My wife and family left me leaving me with nothing'; 'Any plans I had were totally disrupted and destroyed'; 'Shattered normal life'; 'Wondered if any girl would ever love me'; and 'I was suicidal, I didn't think that there was a future.' A similar negative picture was painted of the impact on employment, although one or two mentioned the support or tolerance they experienced at work. Typical responses were: 'Took six months off then was asked to resign'; 'Unable to return to paid work'; 'Gave up when problems started'; 'Got suspended from work until I agreed to get psychiatric help'; or 'In ruins'. Likewise those commenting on the impact on self-confidence portrayed a bleak view: 'An extreme reduction from total self-confidence to no confidence'; 'Became afraid to do things'; 'Completely shattered, feel like a second class citizen'; 'Destroyed'; and 'Can no longer trust people and have no will to live'.

Some of the comments about self-confidence alluded to loss of trust in others or even feelings of persecution by them. When asked more explicitly about friends the following responses were typical: 'Put up barricades to friendship to stop being hurt'; 'Never made friends properly after'; 'Lost many friends'; 'Had to break off friendships'; 'No social life or feelings of any sort'. Relationships with family members were affected in more complex ways, though. Some made similar comments to those about friends and added the notion that the family had caused their problems. However, others talked more favourably about how their problems had brought them closer to their relatives. Thus at one extreme there were comments like, 'They don't take my feelings seriously and they treat me like a leper', and at the other extreme were comments like, 'The relationships were enhanced. They became more caring and supportive.' In the case of the negative statements, three themes emerged: lack of support; loss or rejection; and increased hostility in the relationships. In the case of the positive comments, the emphasis was on the appreciation of care and support.

The longer-term financial impact of mental health problems will be discussed later, but some comment will be made here about the initial impact from the open-ended responses. Understandably the negative comments about employment tied in closely to the financial picture drawn by the respondents. At best there were comments like: 'Not affected because already on a pension.' These were in the minority. The bulk of the responses were of this type: 'From £8,100 pa to £47 pw'; 'Deteriorated considerably'; 'Lost my livelihood completely'; and 'Have to exist on decreased income'.

The open-ended questions about initial contact with services and views on what led to problems resulted in the following types of description, which demonstrate the complexity or variability of understanding patients had about themselves. As we will discuss at greater length later, it is notable that this complexity contrasts with the narrower constructions imposed by psychiatric diagnosis ('mentally ill', 'schizophrenia', 'reactive depression', and so on). Moreover, given that these descriptions are so diverse, it would seem highly implausible that any single solution to emotional distress (be it medical or otherwise) is actually tenable. Note how the mixed list of responses sometimes entails firm views about causality, whilst at other times descriptions are merely given and perplexity remains about any pertinent antecedent events.

In order to highlight the ways in which patients sometimes only described a series of events but at other times alluded to a variety of life circumstances surrounding their initial problem, we quote below a long and random list of different responses.

Doctor put me on anti-depressants and when they weren't working I was referred to a psychiatrist and went into hospital on the same day. I stayed there for seven weeks the first time. This was with my knowledge and agreement throughout.

I went round to my mum's for Christmas and the police were there waiting for me in the house. I had become very ill and my mum was ashamed. I was sectioned and kept in hospital for six months.

My cousin called the social services. The social worker called and arranged for me to see a psychiatrist even though at that time I was already seeing the GP for my problems and he did not refer me to a psychiatrist.

When I woke up I saw a nurse and realised I was in hospital. After about a day I realised it was a mental hospital.

The social worker arranged for me to go into hospital. She knew my home circumstances and thought that it would make matters worse if I went home instead.

I was admitted to hospital after a domiciliary visit by my GP. The GP initiated contact with hospital after a call from my parents.

I was manic at the time, although I did not realise it. I was abroad on a business trip and I went completely 'bananas'. According to the psychiatrist who saw me I was suffering from paranoid delusions. My employer told me that he thought that I was ill and a psychiatrist came to see me that evening.

I was manic and my brother arranged an appointment with a top London doctor.

Police picked me up when they thought I had a drug problem and mistakenly put me in a police cell before being taken to hospital. The police behaved unethically.

My step mother thought I was going to get violent when I picked up a knife. I was feeling paranoid and thought that people were hiding things from me. My dad called the police and a doctor and they came and sectioned me.

Lost job and I became a recluse. Mother informed the doctor when I refused to 'sign on' one morning.

I was engaged to a girl and two weeks before the wedding she broke it off. I cut my throat in her parents' house. Prior to this my mother threatened to cut me off if I married the girl. Tensions caused by this caused rows between me and my fiancée, which left me feeling confused and very hurt.

I had been sexually abused by my father since I was seven. I coped until the death of my grandfather when I was aged nineteen. Then I began to talk about it and get depressed. When I told my husband he began to abuse me. I just couldn't handle this after being abused for so long before.

Stress due to promotion and second marriage — fear of failure of both at the same time.

Me not caring about myself and society not caring about me.

The direct issue was the loss of my baby. The indirect one was problems with my neighbours and my job.

Family stress due to my mother's illness led to me having hallucinations.

Drug abuse led to hallucinations.

Long periods of unemployment. Society in general saying that there was plenty of work to be had, so those out of work were seen as being lazy. Employers told you that you were no good by not employing you.

I was depressed and upset following the death of my mother. We had a difficult relationship and I never felt wanted by her. While she was alive I felt that she never loved me. After her death there was no chance to put that right. Also earlier abuse by a family member affected me and the relationship I had with my husband as a result.

Working back, then, from the impact on their lives, the respondents were asked about who they first discussed their problem with and how helpful the experience was. Table 2.3 shows the range of people involved.

Table 2.3   To whom did the respondents talk?

First person talked to	%
Family doctor	34.5
Family member	21.8
Psychiatrist	20.3
Friend	8.2
Social worker	3.7
Other	11.5

$N = 487$

If the psychiatrists, social workers and GPs are added together, it can be seen that (leaving aside any other profession in the 'other' category) over half of the sample did not have any initial discussion about their problem in the 'lay' area (with friends or relatives). There was a gender bias here, with more women using informal contacts than men within the sample (58 and 42 per cent respectively). A variety of explanations could account for why a majority of the respondents (overall across gender) did not use informal contacts. Most of the sample (63.4 per cent) were single at the time of their first problem, and thus many of them may have been socially isolated, meaning that professional scrutiny may have offered the first opportunity (or imposition?) which led to a discussion. Also, some of the group may not have recognised at the time that they had a problem. It may be that they were a problem to others, who brought in the professionals to interview the putative patient.

As was indicated earlier, perhaps some people also present their distress indirectly, and so do not converse directly with people about their difficulties. Once in the system, professional interviews are then imposed on them, which they may or may not find useful. Those who are involved at this stage in discussions and who are deemed by patients to be helpful are not necessarily the same thing. There is also a question about to what extent these early discussions were found to be helpful. Information about these aspects of the early discussions with others are presented below. Table 2.4 shows to what extent patients found that their first discussion of the problem was of help.

Table 2.4   To what extent did the first person contacted help?

Extent person helped	%
Very helpful	30.3
Helpful	28.9
Neither helpful/unhelpful	21.4
Unhelpful	8.9
Very unhelpful	10.3

$N = 485$

Table 2.4 suggests that, overall, discussion with others in the early phase of the problem was helpful (59.2 per cent). This would support the views of professionals arguing for crisis intervention work with their clients. It also might support the view held by many users that early access to supportive informal networks are important. However, around 40 per cent of the people responding to this question did not benefit by early discussion with others, suggesting that they would have preferred to be left alone or that they would have preferred something other than what was offered.

When further questions were asked about this early helping process, the following picture emerged about parties in the lay area. Both employers and relatives were deemed to be more helpful than friends, with 45, 44 and 30 per cent respectively in these groups being described as either helpful or very helpful. As can be seen, all three groups fail to get a clear commendation from patients, suggesting that the majority of others are either not found to be helpful or are actively alienated from patients. The following qualitative data highlights the positive and negative aspects of these relationships with others.

From an early age I felt under a great deal of pressure, mainly from my family and living circumstances. This caused me to rebel, and made me want to get back at people in general. I got into serious trouble with the police and was put into psychiatric care...I had a violent argument with my father, who hit me. When this happened I ran away and I felt that I wanted to get back at somebody. The first person I met began also to shout at me, so I took my revenge on him...My family didn't want to listen when I had problems...Some neighbours would take me and my sisters in at times and give us cups of tea till my father got home.

I was paranoid – scared of something that might happen to me at work and at home. I thought that I was being watched and the room was bugged. My mother contacted the GP who called out the crisis intervention team...They came and were helpful...my friends, etc., turned their back on my problems.

I had pressure from family and studying. Three years before I contacted a doctor. My mother listened and tried to comfort but my father did not understand...Found friends very supportive when they understood what was happening.

I had depression and phobias leading to attempted suicide...My doctor and family didn't understand me or help but my close friends were prepared to listen and to believe me.

After my mother died, I suffered epileptic fits and violent outbursts...My sister took over my mother's role and took total care of me when I was ill...all the family took responsibility for looking after me. They were very caring.

After being unemployed for a long time I got very depressed and tried to commit suicide...My wife took me to the GP who was very helpful...My wife supported me and stood by me...the rest of the family were also supportive, nobody told me to snap out of it...

After coming out of hospital I stopped seeing my friends and became a recluse.

I got depressed after having the baby...I also had an unsettled marriage and was not used to living in the country...I was left alone on a farm and didn't see my family...My neighbour also had depression after a baby and she advised me to seek medical help.

My problems were caused by the strain of the harassment from my sister and mother. They were no help...My friends just acted as though I had the plague.

I had behaviour problems due to poor upbringing...when explaining my problems to the doctor she just laughed at me so I walked out and wouldn't go back...My family did not care about me or my problems...Other people knew what my problems were but they wouldn't stop and do anything about them or try and understand me.

Mental health problems take varying amounts of time to build up before outside professional intervention is sought. During these build-up periods, there may be successful or unsuccessful attempts at resolution with or without the help of others. Table 2.5 shows something of this build-up. It shows the amount of time taken before problems are taken out of the lay area and presented to professionals. (Note that it does not indicate who was mainly responsible for this shift of focus; that information is presented in Table 2.6.)

Table 2.5   Length of time before consulting a professional

Time before problem taken to professionals	%
1 week	23.3
1–4 weeks	17.2
1–3 months	14.1
3–6 months	13.0
6 months to 1 year	9.3
1–3 years	11.0
Over 3 years	12.1

$N = 454$

This indicates a wide range of time before mental health problems became defined as mental illness as a result of professional intervention. Whilst this process occurs within a month in about 40 per cent of the cases, in over one-fifth of cases it did not take place for over a year. This confirms what has been known from a number of community surveys: there is a gap between those formally labelled as patients and as ill, and a whole sub-population in the community who have mental health problems but who are not 'on the psychiatric books'. It would appear that the respondents were part of that larger sub-group until their psychiatric career started at the point when professionals became involved.

So who is responsible for starting to convert people with distressed or distressing conduct into psychiatric patients with mental illnesses? Only just over one-third of the respondents (34.3 per cent) indicated that they sought professional help alone. In nearly two-thirds of cases this was done by others (50.5 per cent) or in conjunction with others (15.2 per cent). At first sight, this may seem to confirm the description given by Goffman[7] of a 'betrayal funnel' in which others conspire with professionals against the incipient patient. However, only 15 per cent of the respondents said that they were unhappy or very unhappy about the role played by others in the contact period, whereas 75 per cent of them described the role of others as being helpful or very helpful. Thus Goffman's betrayal funnel may well exist, but only in a minority of cases. Of course, when it does exist serious moral and political questions are then raised, appropriately, about the rights of those 'conspired against'. (These will be addressed later in Chapter 7, in relation to the problems surrounding informed consent.)

Table 2.6 describes who was the main link person with mental health services once professional contact was made. It is clear that GPs play a pivotal role in this contact. This is hardly surprising as they are the main gatekeepers for all specialist services inside the NHS. What may be surprising to readers not familiar with research on the role of the police as gatekeepers (informally and under Section 136 of the Mental Health Act) is their regular involvement in mental health crises. Although this was reported below in only 8 per cent of cases, this is still twice the rate of involvement of a more familiar link, the social worker. Consequently, perhaps the police should be thought of as 'frontline' mental health workers.

Table 2.6   Identity of main link with mental health services

Link person with mental health services	%
GP	59.9
Police	8.0
Family member	7.0
Psychiatrist	6.4
Social worker	4.0
Friend	1.8
Other	9.4
More than one of above	3.5

$N = 501$

Differences between male and female responses

The discussion of the data up to now has made little distinction between male and female responses. The two groups do depict their early experiences differently, although (not surprisingly) there is a large overlap. For instance, both groups identified bereavement and the stress of studying as being relevant to the development of their problems in equal numbers. This was also the case for those respondents who attributed their early difficulties simply to mental illness. Their was no difference found between male and female respondents in relation to levels of satisfaction with GP treatment, attitude and information. In this sample there were no significant differences in the number of visits to their GP. (This is a little surprising as other studies suggest that women have greater GP contact than men and discussion of the 'minor tranquilliser' problem has often focused on women.) Also, both groups reported similar levels of satisfaction with the helpfulness of friends and employers. Half the numbers of both men and women were given a diagnosis on admission to hospital, and both groups felt equal levels of satisfaction about the necessity of admission.

In other respects, though, a discrepant picture emerged. Of 50 respondents indicating that marital stress was the source of their difficulties, 31 were women and 19 were men. By contrast men reported work stress to be of relevance three times more often than did women. This could be accounted for by the fact that there is a traditional division between men and women in the domestic and work arenas. Women may attach greater meanings to relationships at home than at work, whereas the reverse is the case with men. In the study by Brown and Harris[8] of depression in working-class women in Camberwell, the role of a close confiding relationship was identified as an important protective factor. Our data confirms that marital breakdown is indeed relevant to both men and women in the development of mental health problems, and that women are more sensitive about this issue than are men. Relationships in the domestic arena seem to take on a greater meaning for women than men. In the long term, the mental health of women actually improves following separation from male partners, whereas the reverse is true for men.[9]

Another traditional difference attributed to women and men is that the former are likely to share emotional difficulties more readily than the latter. This is confirmed by the data. Of 89 respondents who chose their lay network of friends as their first attempt to seek help, 52 were women and 37 were men. By contrast, of 108 people using a professional as their 'first port of call' with their difficulty, 64 were men and 44 were women. As well as women possibly having a greater learned facility to share problems with others at an earlier stage, men may consider it not 'macho' to declare weakness in the lay area. A professional consultation with a stranger may thus come more easily. In part this may also account for why men are more likely to report feeling coerced by non-professionals more often than women, although there was no difference between the groups in terms of rates of reported formal compulsory detention ('sectioning') under the Mental Health Act.

Age of the respondents

As with sex, the age of the respondents appears to be relevant in some respects but not others. For instance, there was no significant difference between age groups in relation to lay and professional help-seeking, or in the levels of helpfulness reported by family members, employers or GPs. However, there were age differences with regard to satisfaction with information from GPs. Of 178 respondents satisfied with this information, 41 per cent were under forty, compared to 59 per cent who were over forty. This was reinforced by a symmetrical picture in reverse. Of 138 respondents who were dissatisfied with GP information, 59 per cent were under forty whereas 41 per cent were over forty. This seems to imply that younger people expect more accurate or satisfactory information than older people from their GP.

This discrepancy between the two age bands may be accounted for by several factors. Younger people may be less accepting and deferential than older people in the face of professional authority. Maybe the NHS is more likely to be seen as a right rather than a privilege by younger people. Differences over time in education between the groups may have led to different expectations about information-seeking. There were no differences between the groups in terms of the reported satisfaction with the attitudes, rather than information, provided by GPs. Thus this would imply that GPs need to review their policy about information giving. A similar picture emerges after admission to hospital. Younger people are significantly more dissatisfied than older people about the explanations given by professionals about their condition. Put crudely, it seems that professionals can fob off older people more easily than they can young people. Maybe both groups are deserving of respect in relation to offering information, and the younger group is signalling this message in the data for patients in general.

Social class

It is well known that a class gradient exists in psychiatric diagnosis. Poorer people are more likely to receive such a label, particularly that of schizophrenia. The controversy about social mobility and downward drift (does mental illness make you poor or does poverty make you mentally ill?) cannot be simply resolved by the data; the survey was not designed to be an epidemiological investigation. However, some points of discussion can be raised.

There were 29 people whose parents were in social classes I–III but who now reported being in classes IV or V. Of this group 20 were male and 9 were female. This may indicate that women are protected from downward drift more often than men by being married. There were also 54 people who started in classes IV or V and subsequently reached classes I–III. This partial evidence of *upward* mobility is in line with some other survey evidence.[10] Comparing these two groups, men were more likely to be downwardly rather than upwardly mobile. Also, downwardly mobile patients were more likely to have been diagnosed as psychotic (27 per cent compared to 18 per cent of the upwardly mobile group). However, it should be emphasised that these mobile groups were in the minority. The majority of the respondents simply stayed in their social class of origin.

The data also suggest that starting in a higher class increases the chances of being in paid work despite being a psychiatric patient. Basically, a more privileged background seems to insulate patients against the vagaries of the system to some extent. Of the 69 (13 per cent) in the sample who described their main income as coming from full or part-time employment, 44 (64 per cent) had fathers from social classes I–III. Also, of those citing their main income as deriving from jobs, 77 per cent were classified as being in classes I–III. This seems to indicate that middle- and upper-class patients are favoured in their employment prospects and maintenance compared to lower-class patients.

As far as early encounters with the psychiatric system are concerned, class differences were not apparent in relation to levels of helpfulness of GPs or in the supply of a diagnosis. Other differences were apparent, however. Lower-class patients were significantly more likely to be pressurised by professionals than their higher-class counterparts. 'Lower-class' patients also enter the system at a significantly younger age, since 85 per cent of the 'lower-class' group reported their problems to have started before the age of 24 compared to 67 per cent of the higher-class patients. 'Higher-class' patients are significantly more likely to feel dissatisfied about information given to them both at the outset and later by professionals. This is consistent with other studies which indicate that expectations about information increase the higher the social class of the patient.

Discussion

This chapter has presented some of the main findings of the survey related to the onset of mental health problems. It has also introduced some theoretical debates about the ways in which these problems are negotiated or constructed by three key parties (patients-to-be, their immediate network and mental health professionals). It is clear that these negotiations are complicated in a number of respects. For a start, they do not arise out of the blue: they are accounted for by the respondents within a life story, much as a person could, for instance, put their career or their sexual relationships into such a personal historical context.

Also, there is no simple or uniform picture about how people understand this account and its context. Their world is not the simple psychiatric one of mentally-ill-versus-not-mentally-ill (only one-tenth of the sample were happy to describe their problems in these terms). It could be argued that this lay view of problems is flawed and inadequate because it is not an expert view. In other words, it may be prevalent in the untrained population but it should be treated as interesting and quaint (that is, given less credence than the view of professionals). This type of defence of accounting for psychiatric patienthood better in medical terms would have some credibility if the illness model in psychiatry had a proven and convincing track record. Unfortunately for psychiatrists it does not, hence the ability of hostile critics, such as Szasz, to develop a credible argument about the myth of mental illness.

The illness model in psychiatry has had four main difficulties in sustaining its credibility. First, despite years of research and vast quantities spent internationally on seeking biological causes (aetiological explanations) for mental illnesses, no agreement has been reached. There is some indication that identifiable social factors which cause stress for people (poverty, loss, social isolation) will make them prone to experiencing versions of fear, sadness and confusion.[11] However, this relationship between stress and distress does not need to be accounted for within an illness framework. So, when people account for their distress in terms of, say, bereavement or study stress, what advantage is there in invoking an illness description? One answer could be that such a diagnostic approach provides us with more accurate information than leaving it to the vague or idiosyncratic notions articulated by patients or others in their lay network. This brings us to the second and third problems with the illness framework.

The second problem is that diagnostic categories have themselves been found to be woolly and incoherent (in the jargon, they lack 'construct validity'). Recently, for instance, taken-for-granted major mental illness labels such as 'schizophrenia' have been criticised for being confused and useless for research purposes.[12]

Linked to this issue of construct validity there is the question of the predictive validity of illness descriptions in psychiatry: if a person receives a diagnostic label does this predict the outcome of their case (in the jargon, is it the best 'prognostic indicator')? The answer is 'no'. It would appear that the long-term course of psychiatric patients' lives (in terms of their improvement, stasis or deterioration) is not well predicted by the diagnosis they are given. Once more, social factors such as job opportunities seem to be better predictors.[13] Thus professional accounts of illness seem to be unconvincing in terms of their validity, so there is no logical reason to favour them over lay accounts.

The third problem with the illness model in psychiatry has been that it is not safe to assume that professionals consistently diagnose in the same way. They have a poor record of agreement (or in research terminology, there is poor 'inter-rater reliability' in psychiatric diagnosis). Given that these diagnoses are suspect on grounds of both validity and reliability, why given them a privileged status?

The fourth difficulty is that in medicine a diagnosis is usually deemed to be worthwhile if it leads to rational predictions about treatment. However, here again the picture is very confused. Take the notion, reported typically in psychiatric literature, that the treatment of choice of schizophrenia has been major tranquillisers. In fact, all sorts of other treatments have also claimed some partial success, including minor tranquillisers and psychotherapy.[14] Similarly, major tranquillisers are given to patients with other diagnoses. The same weak relationship (between diagnosis and treatment offered) is seen in most of the other diagnostic categories used by psychiatrists.

These problems with the illness model in psychiatry have been rehearsed in summary form in order to highlight whether professional accounts really have any claim to superiority in understanding or explaining mental health problems. Other ways of talking about the experiences attached to these problems arguably are better than traditional psychiatric descriptions. The very fact that the respondents in our study came up with such a long list of attributions, together with a large 'other' category, may indicate that patients have a more complex and sophisticated range of descriptive or explanatory frameworks than psychiatrists with their notion of 'mental illness'.

In the light of this common gap between lay and professional understanding of mental health problems, what do patients make of what is done to them by psychiatric experts? It is this question that we address next.

References

1. Szasz, T. S., *The Myth of Mental Illness* (New York: Harper & Row, 1961).
2. Laing, R. D. and Esterson, A., *Sanity, Madness and the Family* (London: Tavistock, 1964).

3. Sedgwick, P. *PsychoPolitics* (London: Pluto Press, 1982).
4. Scott, R. D., 'The Treatment Barrier (Part I)', *British Journal of Medical Psychology*, 46, 45 (1973).
5. Coulter, J. *Approaches to Insanity* (London: Martin Robinson, 1973).
6. Goffman, E., *Asylums* (Harmondsworth: Penguin, 1961).
7. Ibid.
8. Brown, G. and Harris, T., *The Social Origins of Depression* (London: Tavistock, 1978).
9. Gove, W.R., 'The Relationship between Sex Roles, Marital Status and Mental Illness', *Social Forces*, 51 (1972), pp. 34–44.
10. Myers, J. and Bean, L., *A Decade Later: A Follow Up of Social Class and Mental Illness* (New York: Wiley, 1968).
11. Newton, J., *The Prevention of Mental Illness* (London, Routledge & Kegan Paul, 1989).
12. Boyle, M., *Schizophrenia: A Scientific Delusion?* (London: Routledge & Kegan Paul, 1990).
13. Warner, R., *Recovery from Schizophrenia: The Political Economy of Psychiatry* (London: Routledge & Kegan Paul, 1985).
14. Bentall, R. P., Jackson, H. and Pilgrim, D., 'Abandoning the Concept of Schizophrenia: Some Implications for Validity Arguments when Studying Psychotic Phenomena', *British Journal of Clinical Psychology*, 27 (1988), pp. 303–24.

3
A Look at the Experts

There are three common and contradictory images of health professionals. The first of these is unambiguously positive and is typified by the selfless heroics of the accident and emergency staff in the popular television series, 'Casualty'. Not only are these doctors and nurses depicted as being dedicated to the needs of patients, but they generally seem to know exactly what they are doing. A second image, which also haunts our culture, is one of people who come to take you away to the 'funny farm' or the 'loony bin'. As in the film 'One Flew Over the Cuckoo's Nest', angry or frightened victims are callously disposed of without a care for their sensitivities or civil rights. After the disposal, they try to survive in a sinister, incarcerated world of forced injections, solitary confinement and habitual brutality and neglect. The third common mythology about the mental health industry entails the assumption that psychiatrists are all psychoanalysts. Consequently, in this imagined world, it is assumed that they are highly skilled in making interpretations, even to the point of being able to 'read minds'. Radio programmes, such as Anthony Clare's 'In The Psychiatrist's Chair', reinforce this notion, as did the Thames Television's soap opera 'Shrinks'. It is obvious that these three professional images do not fit easily together.

The first image is constructed by those committed to a simple progressive view of state-funded health care delivery, in which staff are over-worked and under-paid carers. The second arises from fears, dating back to images of Bedlam, of unjustified loss of liberty and assault from agents of the state. Consequently, liberal and libertarian social commentators of both right and left have been alert to these fears being or becoming a practical reality. The third image bears little relationship to typical interventions in state-provided Anglo–American psychiatry. Psychoanalytical psychotherapy is only a minority pursuit in the NHS. However, programmes such as Clare's reinforce the assumptions of the uninitiated that an encounter with a psychiatrist typically involves a lengthy empathic exploration of the patient's biography.

So, to get these images into perspective, what evidence is available? Some derives from official statistics. For instance, we know from these that about 10 per cent of in-patients are in hospital against their will under a section of the 1983 Mental Health Act. Consequently, it would be very surprising if at least the same percentage of our respondents did not complain about the 'jailer' role of mental health professionals. What is probable from this scale of involuntary detention of patients is that the first unambiguously positive image of staff, sketched above, is unlikely to prevail amongst psychiatric patients. Although there is legislation to incarcerate physically ill people forcibly (the National Assistance Act) this is used much less frequently than the Mental Health Act. Moreover, even under this lesser-used legislation, many of the patients detained are elderly and dementing, so may well be diagnosed as suffering from an organic mental illness by a psychiatrist. Thus it is obvious that the life-saving efforts of staff in the acute medical sector, responding to physical illness or injury, can be depicted more readily as heroic and benign than is the case with mental health professionals.

It was already clear, from the data discussed in Chapter 2, that the respondents have mixed views about whether the 'conspiracy model' with its 'betrayal funnel' does actually provide an accurate account of their early psychiatric experiences. What this chapter will explore in more detail is to what extent the respondents considered that mental health professionals complied with the three over-drawn cultural myths described above. The focus will be on what patients say about the mental health professionals they encountered during their in-patient and out-patient time.

The in-patient experience of experts

First, a comparative view of professionals by patients will be considered. They were asked who helped most and least during their in-patient stay, and the results are shown in Tables 3.1 and 3.2.

When interpreting these tables it has to be remembered that these open-ended comparisons are not based upon equal contact with each of the groups listed. Only psychiatrists and nurses (and other patients) are likely to have been encountered by all of the respondents. Consequently, these two professional groups are

Table 3.1　Who helped most?

Who helped most?	%
Nurses	32.4
Patients	12.7
Psychiatrists	12.1
Social workers	11.8
Friends	5.5
Partner	4.8
Psychologists	4.8
Family	8.2
Psychotherapists	3.5
Other	4.2

N = 456

Table 3.2　Who helped least?

Who helped least?	%
Psychiatrists	21.3
Social workers	17.7
Nurses	10.0
Family	6.9
Friends	6.7
Partner	6.5
Patients	5.9
Psychotherapists	3.5
Psychologists	3.3
Other	18.2

N = 508

likely to be singled out by patients for comment (both positive and negative). Lesser contacted professionals (like psychologists) are accordingly mentioned in only a minority of cases in both tables.

It impossible to gauge accurately what level of contact did exist with the other groups. For instance, not all psychiatric patients are referred to psychologists and, in another case, social workers have both the role of helping informally and also of taking a high profile, albeit briefly, in the coercive 'sectioning' of admitted patients. This may be reflected in the mixed view of them appearing in the two tables. Thus it is difficult to pin down the implication of the number of positive and negative responses related to these 'paramedical' professionals. It is because psychiatric nurses and psychiatrists are the two core care professionals involved in dealing with in-patients that these will be the focus of the rest of the chapter.

Psychiatric nurses

Patients in hospital are cared for around the clock by shifts of nurses. This puts the nurses in a peculiar position of being constant, as opposed to sporadic, carers (the status of other 'nine to five' professionals). However, it has to be emphasised that this constant care role is a collective responsibility of the profession, as individual nurses move in and out from shift to shift. Nonetheless, nurses constitute the backbone of in-patient care, so the quality of their work is very important for patients. Table 3.3 indicates, in general terms, what the respondents commenting on their nursing care thought of this quality.

Table 3.3   Amount of satisfaction with nursing care

Satisfaction with nursing care	%
Very satisfied	25.5
Satisfied	33.9
Neutral	18.9
Dissatisfied	10.7
Very dissatisfied	10.9

$N = 475$

Overall, these figures suggest that the profession is looked upon favourably by patients, but the 40 per cent who did not consider nursing care to be satisfactory again imply that complacency is not warranted. This general evaluation is fleshed out by the qualitative data on the best and worst experiences of nursing care. These map out what patients considered to be good and bad models of practice.

Good nursing practice

Respectful and empathic listening

Below are some examples of the most favoured aspect of care, that of ordinary contact which is respectful and empathic:

> When I was a day patient there was a very caring nurse. She never talked down to me. She always treated me as an equal and I always trusted her to tell me whether I was making progress or deteriorating. Basically, I trusted her.

> There was a young trainee nurse who spent time talking to me. She naturally had empathy with me and at the end of listening to my tale, of 23 years, she gave me a big hug.

> Warm empathy experienced when I was just coming out of psychosis. It was really nice to meet a caring nurse who I could talk to at this point.

> My key worker spent much time talking with me. He got into trouble about this.

Good physical care

Another valued aspect of nursing was of direct physical care.

> A nice male nurse helped me with my toothache.

> I had two heart attacks while in hospital and on both occasions the nurses resuscitated me.

> Being fed meals.

One male patient intriguingly reported an experience which was highly valued and memorable but was probably also unethical: 'I was seduced by a female nurse when out on a walk locally.' Other patients emphasised more general qualities of dedicated and helpful attitudes from nurses. Not surprisingly, the negative experiences were more lengthy or were charged with more emotion. As with any other experiences in life, untoward events tend to be more noteworthy. So, without losing sight of the backing generally given to the nursing staff in Table 3.3, the following responses describe how nurses should not conduct themselves in the opinion of psychiatric patients.

Bad nursing practice

Prioritising professional needs

The first group of responses emphasise the ways in which nurses put their own needs first:

> The night staff were evil. They hated it if you ever disturbed them from their sleep.

> Nurses just wanted to comply with regulations or instructions. They didn't care about my needs.

> Some nurses are excellent but a lot seem to be just doing it for a job.

> Most of them don't care about the patients.

Cruelty and authoritarianism

Another group of responses related to cruel or authoritarian attitudes:

> At one hospital I found the nurses strict and regimental. They pushed me around a bit.

> They didn't treat me right. They didn't make feel as though I was wanted. Female nurses were worse than the males in this regard.

> After I was re-admitted once when I took my own discharge, the Sister said 'You didn't last very long.' Some of the nurses were like dictators.

> One sister used to treat me like I was sub-human and while in the heights of mania she would not listen to my pleas for help.

> After I took an overdose, the staff nurse asked me if the stomach pump had been greased. When I said it had, she said that she would have left it ungreased because people taking overdoses should suffer.

Physical assualt

The following responses reported abuse, sometimes but not always related to forced physical 'treatment'. The report of forced injections was a common complaint.

A group of nurses forced me to have an injection I didn't want.

I was punched in the face when I refused to take my tablets.

I was given heavy medication then stripped and left locked up in a room for several days. I cried and cried but they would not let me out.

Being forcibly returned to hospital even though I was a voluntary patient.

Two or three nurses were very violent to me once and dragged me by the hair.

So these open-ended responses were very varied. At one end of the spectrum were comments such as, 'Psychiatric nurses are totally dedicated and the best caring staff you could want'; at the other end of the spectrum were the above complaints of abuse. In between were summaries, such as 'They are not a single group. They range from appalling to being extremely helpful', or 'Some are very good and others very bad. Some are more institutionalised than the patients.'

Psychiatrists

It is understandable that psychiatrists are expected to respond to patients in a special way. After all, within the mental health industry, psychiatry is the dominant profession with the highest status and remuneration. As a consequence it even gives its name ('psychiatric care') to a whole multi-disciplinary effort. Due to the expectations this central role encourages, users of psychiatric services are likely to hold the medical profession particularly responsible for the quality of the service they experience. In this light, and with our shared cultural myths discussed earlier in mind, psychiatrists came under justifiable critical scrutiny from the respondents.

The psychoanalytical image of the profession may well lead patients to assume that their encounters with consultant psychiatrists will be frequent (even daily), of long duration, and that they will focus on biographical details. The respondents did not find this to be the case in practice. Table 3.4 summarises the frequency of private contact reported by in-patients.

Table 3.4   Frequency of contact with consultants (in-patient)

In-patient contact with consultant	%
Once a day	4.9
Once a week	38.7
Once a month	14.4
Every three months	2.7
Once a year	2.2
Never	37.1

$N = 448$

Only around 5 per cent of those responding to this question reported seeing their consultant psychiatrist alone daily. Weekly contact was experienced by less than 40 per cent of the respondents, so arguably only around four out of ten patients see their psychiatrist alone with sufficient regularity for their doctor to make decisions based on reasonably up-to-date knowledge of the patients' condition. This leaves around 60 per cent being treated by consultants whose personalised contact varies from monthly to 'never'. This question was about individual contact, so the 'never' contact does not necessarily imply that their consultants were totally unknown to them. It does indicate clearly, though, that over one-third of patients do not receive individualised interview sessions with their consultants. How does this compare to those reporting on their level of out-patient contact? These results are shown in Table 3.5.

Table 3.5   Frequency of contact with psychiatrists (out-patient)

Out-patient contact with psychiatrist	%
Weekly	12.8
Monthly	35.3
3-monthly	37.3
6-monthly	7.0
Yearly	7.6

$N = 399$

The out-patient reports indicate that, cumulatively, patients see more of their psychiatrist in a three-month period when they are out of hospital than in. Of course, these relatively low levels of contact are only descriptions of reported frequencies. In themselves they say nothing about the perceived usefulness of the meetings for patients, and neither do they indicate the length of each interview (see Table 3.6).

Table 3.6   Length of interviews with psychiatrists

Estimated duration of each interview	%
0–5 mins	16.4
6–20 mins	54.2
21–35 mins	16.6
36–60 mins	10.3
Over 60 mins	2.5

$N = 408$

From Table 3.6, it can be seen that less than one-third of the respondents reported interview times of more than 20 minutes with their consultants, with only 2.5 per cent seeing their doctors for an hour or more. Less than half of the respondents (41.3 per cent) reported meetings being held at their request. These findings, plus the tables reporting frequency of contact above, indicate quite clearly that most psychiatrists do not behave like psychoanalysts as far as time spent with patients is concerned.

What, then, did the respondents have to say about the content of their contact with their treating psychiatrists? Only half (49.8 per cent) thought that psychiatrists were easy to talk to. A similar picture emerged of the respondents' views on the helpfulness of psychiatrists: 54.7 per cent thought that they were helpful or very helpful. When the respondents were asked about information and explanations in the interviews with their doctors, they moved from this narrow vote of confidence to a more critical appraisal. Only 34.4 per cent were satisfied with the explanation given to them by psychiatrists about their condition. Only 20.0 per cent were satisfied with the information they were given during these encounters about their treatment. To confirm this, only 16.6 per cent were satisfied with the information they were given on side-effects of treatment. To summarise, Table 3.7 shows levels of satisfaction with the overall attitude of psychiatrists.

Table 3.7   Levels of satisfaction with psychiatrist's attitude

Attitude of psychiatrist	%
Very helpful	14.3
Helpful	30.7
Neutral	16.6
Unhelpful	26.1
Very unhelpful	12.3

$N = 463$

Taking all the above data together, it would seem that psychiatrists barely reach a majority vote of confidence from the respondents. Depending on how the question is posed, this confidence varies from a small majority (54.7 per cent on helpfulness) to less than half (45 per cent on attitude). This poor showing of psychiatrists is deemed to be even worse when the information and explanations they give out are evaluated by patients.

The following qualitative data enlarges the above picture.

Good medical practice

The following comments highlight what psychiatrists need to model on, as far as good practice is concerned:

Very good generally. Explained things right from the beginning when asked.

They understand my problems and they have always given me an appointment when I've asked for one.

It took many years for them to discuss properly with me my illness, diagnosis and medication. But now they have done so it has been very helpful. They are always there if I need them.

These quotations draw attention to three crucial 'user-friendly' aspects of psychiatric practice. First, doctors should be empathic in the eyes of patients. Second, they should be willing and able to share all the information and explanations available to them with the person in their care. Third, they should be accessible to patients on the latter's terms. This is captured by the recent users' movement slogan of professionals needing to be 'On tap not on top!'

Bad medical practice

The negative comments about treatment at the hands of psychiatrists reflect an inversion of the above good practices.

> I felt that there has been little understanding of my problems and more of an emphasis on drugs and prescriptions.

> Acted as though it's not their problem. Often don't seem to care at all. Felt like they were always twisting everything you said.

> They appear unconcerned about the problem. They come across as being more interested in what they have to say about the problem than what the patient has to say.

> Lacked understanding of my problems. Quite rude about things I couldn't do and humiliated me in front of other people. No bedside manner.

Disliked psychiatrists are reported as being distant and uninvolved in a helping relationship:

> They are passive. They don't provide any information regarding prognosis, diagnosis and treatment. They appear to be unimaginative and unsympathetic.

> They won't say anything. They are dummies. I get more help talking to a stranger at a bus stop because at least you can communicate with them.

> Reserved, detached, godly.

> Condescending, complacent benevolence.

They are reported to be preoccupied with their own professional objectives of social control or experimentation with their favoured physical treatments rather than with the needs of the patient.

They have a set diagnosis which they work to and treat with ECT and drugs. They do not search out the reasons for your illness with you so the illness just repeats again and again.

I feel that I was treated too much as an object rather than a person.

They try to rule your life and make you into a different person.

Authoritarian, aggressive, controlling, suppressive, judgmental, overly clinical and provided containment rather than support.

Why are professionals damned with faint praise?

Our data has allowed us to begin to understand how psychiatric patients evaluate hospital doctors and nurses. Due to the variable role of others such as social workers and psychologists, we can be less sure of the implications of the responses. So, in this discussion section, we will discuss the data in respect of the largest of the two groups of psychiatric staff.

It is clear that, whilst good personal qualities and desirable professional practices are identified, these mental health workers still come under substantial attack. Why is this? The possibilities considered below could account for the criticisms.

Mental illness

The views could be dismissed on grounds of lack of informant competence due to mental illness. We have discussed and dismissed this as being untenable earlier. It could be that these views are from a biased sample of self-selected critics. Again, whilst this is logically possible, it is unlikely. As the methodological appendix shows, there are no strong grounds for believing that our respondents were particularly atypical. Also, their comments are not wholly critical. It is more accurate to say that they damn professionals with faint praise rather than dismiss them out of hand.

Psychiatry is an imperfect science

Another explanation for the disgruntled picture from users is that psychiatry is an imperfect science or art, and that it is difficult for professionals to 'get it right', given their present state of knowledge. This would be a fair defence but it is not common in practice. On the contrary, psychiatric professionals diagnose and prescribe with much the same confidence as other 'experts'. An example of this is their readiness to label people as 'schizophrenic' even though the diagnosis is conceptually weak and has poor predictive validity.

Thus it is important to highlight the possible gap between actual competence (in terms of knowledge about 'aetiology' and efficacy of treatment) and claimed competence. It may be that much of the reticence to communicate complained of by the respondents is a function of psychiatrists not really being certain of what they are doing, or being unable to give a credible account of their competence or knowledge.

Fear of telling the truth

Added to this reluctance to admit their ignorance, psychiatrists may have an anxiety about confessing what they *do* know. An example of this is their unwillingness to admit that commonly used forms of treatment, such as major tranquillisers, are actually very powerful and dangerous. They can induce a variety of transient and permanent side-effects, which are distressing or disabling.

To be accurate, although we retain here the everyday use of the term 'side-effects', realistically they are *effects* of the drugs: effects which are undesirable, and at times even more disabling than the 'illness' they are treating. In this light, the most obvious reason why patients complain of not being given enough information about side-effects could be that psychiatrists are fearful of telling the truth about what they know. Consequently, much of the time they do not admit to their patients the known dangers associated with the treatments they prescribe. The respondents may simply be complaining, quite accurately, about diffidence on the part of professionals to admit what is known about the iatrogenic (drug-induced) effects of, say, major tranquillisers.

Indeed, in a recent small study on patient satisfaction in a Coventry psychiatric unit,[1] the researchers (who were psychiatrists) reported the problem of informed consent about treatment.

Their stance on this was not to demand that a policy on information-giving should be revised radically by their profession. Instead, they rehearsed the conventional caution of not raising patients' anxiety by imparting news about potential side-effects.

Thus paternalism may prevent doctors from being candid with their patients. Their fear of worrying patients is a commonly heard refrain or rationalisation about why they are economical with the truth. However, a price is paid for this paternalism. Patients are denied access to information about treatments which could affect their well-being. Moreover, in the wake of this experience of being 'kept in the dark', patients will quite understandably feel patronised, deceived and aggrieved, which is reflected in the data.

Social control

A fourth source of disaffection with professionals, bearing in mind the reported image of criticised doctors and nurses, is that they are actually simply doing their job. They are employed primarily to tidy up a particular form of deviance, which is understandable neither in terms of criminal intent nor physical illness. This 'residual deviance' is, in essence, what is legally called 'mental disorder' and is clinically called 'mental illness'. One consequence of the tidying up task is that those mental health professionals who have formal legal powers of detention are obliged, at times, to deprive people of their liberty. Accordingly, they are agents of social control acting on behalf of both their state employers and the everyday moral order (of relatives and the public) to remove offensive citizens.

Legislation, such as the 1983 Mental Health Act, exists specifically to make this process a legitimate enterprise on the part of doctors, social workers and nurses. This power is rarely highlighted by professionals, for obvious reasons. Like other state-employed 'helping professions', doctors, nurses and social workers are supposed to be involved in caring for or curing people. Understandably, they may be reluctant to admit a more oppressive role, either to themselves or their patients. However, such coyness and self-deception does not alter the reality of the quasi-penal role of psychiatry in modern society. No matter how much forced incarceration is dressed up paternalistically as 'treatment', at the end of the day it is still forced incarceration.

Thus what patients complain about in the conduct of professionals may actually be about the latter simply conforming to a traditional role set for them. Psychiatrists began as superintendents of lunatic asylums in the Victorian period, with asylum attendants (now nurses) being employed to man-handle the mad. Such a role was essentially about 'warehousing' and physically controlling madness.[2] Alongside that role was an assumption that mental disorder was clearly a brain disease, whose aetiological secret had still to be unlocked. This presumed biological cause is still influential in psychiatric thought today. Consequently, personal sensitivity was never a high priority in the treatment of madness by doctors. Instead, there was and remains a preoccupation with the 'obligation' to treat an impersonal disease process. After the First World War, with psychological treatments being added to psychiatric practice,[3] the public increasingly began to expect something akin to psycho-analysis in their encounters with psychiatrists. In fact, the old biological treatments have remained the dominant medical response in practice. A gap therefore began to open up between the expectation that psychiatrists would pay heed to the patient's biography at length, and the experience of more typical biological treatments, which only require a much more cursory interview. In the latter, the patient's communications are only of interest to doctors in revealing symptoms, not in terms of them being personally meaningful and the basis for shared exploration in a therapeutic relationship. This historical picture helps us to understand why some doctors and nurses behave in cursory, coercive and impersonal way at times, and why patients object to such conduct.

Conclusion

This chapter has described what our respondents thought of the specialist professionals they encountered in the psychiatric system. In particular, good and bad medical and nursing practices have been identified. We have also rehearsed some possible explanations for why staff may at times act in a manner which is offensive to users. The whole question of paternalism and lack of respect will be highlighted again in Chapter 7, when we consider whether psychiatric patients really are consenting adults. The users' views of professionals presented above will be discussed further in the next chapter and placed in a wider context of what the respondents thought of the psychiatric services they encountered.

4
Whose Service?

The policy background to the survey data

One of the problems of trying to evaluate good practice in mental health services is the lack of specific aims and objectives associated with current mental health policy. One can safely say that there is a general consensus about moving from a system of warehousing people in the large Victorian asylums to 'care in the community'. However, over and above this global objective, there appear to be few agreed principles about the look of a post-institutional world.

The present philosophy underlying mental health planning seems *ad hoc* rather than coherent; full of good intentions but not fully worked out. Whilst the most recent central government policy document on mental health[1] has been identified as being broadly 'client-centred' in orientation,[2] it contains little in the way of models or philosophy to ensure good practice. The reason for this appears to be a reluctance on the part of the Department of Health to be prescriptive. Instead, broad objectives of a mental health service are suggested, such as it being comprehensive, locally integrated and flexible.[3] In principle this could encourage a genuine, local, 'bottom-up' form of planning, which elicits the specific needs of mental health consumers. However, to date such a trend is not strongly evident. Most district policy statements go no further than making generalised statements about requirements to serve the 'mental health needs' of the local population. Rather than going on to explore in an open-ended way the particular needs of individuals in terms of employment, social opportunities and networks, the content of many regional and district plans are littered with generalised statements about the 'needs of the mentally ill'. These are usually translated myopically into the number of beds required per thousand population or places in day hospitals. Little notice is usually taken of the local social context or resources outside the immediate confines of health service facilities.

Even the widely agreed aim of providing 'community care' is not a very accurate or useful portrayal of the reality of present mental health services. Mental health provision in Britain is still overwhelmingly hospital based. Although the number of psychiatric beds has decreased overall from 193 000 in 1959 to 108 000 in 1985, there has been a rise in the number of small psychiatric hospitals. During this period the number of psychiatric hospitals actually increased, from 303 to 492.[4] Moreover, despite a steady decline in the number of people occupying hospital beds since the 1960s, short-stay admissions have risen dramatically,[5] creating 'revolving door' hospital care rather than genuine community care.

Much of 'new' mental health provision has simply been transferred to local DGH sites. Day hospitals, together with psychiatric units, are for many localities the back bone of new 'community services'. Warnings that such developments were unlikely to improve matters have been ignored. George Brown, for example,[6] cautioned against re-institutionalisation almost two decades ago on the basis that 'association with the general hospital in itself seems particularly lame as a solution. Such hospitals have continually to struggle to balance technical efficiency and humane care' (p.407). Research has also indicated that DGH psychiatric unit settings do not necessarily lead to better links with the local community or improvements in the therapeutic environment.[7]

Thus, rather than re-provision involving the changing of the content and nature of services, a policy of 'transhospitalisation' has been occurring; patients simply go to a new hospital rather than an old one. This in part may be due to the failure to take on board a radical critique of the oppression of psychiatric patients in asylums. This critique has explored the nature of psychiatric treatment and power relations which exist between users and professionals. In this the British experience contrasts starkly with reforms elsewhere. In Italy, for example, the recognition of the dynamics of oppression between doctor and patient and a political critique of institutionalisation was central to changing mental health policy.[8] Instead, British conservatism and pragmatism has dominated the planning of mental health services. Mental health is rarely viewed as a social, let alone a political, problem. When dominant psychiatric interests are faced with inevitable social change (such as the closure of large hospitals) they react by seeking new sites on which to practice their old ways (a point we will return to in the final chapter).

Outside DGH psychiatric units there has, in some areas, been a rapid development of other community resources.[9] However, recent commentators have suggested that such services have tended to adopt hospital-dominated practices and philosophies.[10] Nonetheless, on the margins, there have been innovations in mental health service delivery. Some locally-based services, mainly in the voluntary sector, working with a tiny percentage of the local mental health budget, have struggled to provide new models of client-centred working.[11] Yet services that do deviate from hospital-based custodial norms are often vulnerable. If they are developed from within the health service, they are often subject to hostility from those who wish to protect more 'traditional' ways of working. As Maxwell Jones pointed out, therapeutic communities in this country provided for orthodox psychiatry 'a name to be wheeled out whenever it wants to defend Britain's reputation as the country which pioneered social psychiatry and to be conveniently forgotten otherwise'.[12] Innovative services are usually subjected to evaluation. Whilst evaluation and 'quality assurance' can be used to promote 'consumer' satisfaction, emerging services are at a disadvantage compared to existing provisions which have not been subject to systematic evaluation and are not deemed to require the same intense scrutiny.

Innovations are also vulnerable to cuts in resources. The Cassel hospital, an NHS psychiatric hospital providing a unique therapeutic community run on psychotherapeutic lines, was recently threatened with closure at a time when many traditional Victorian Hospitals are slowing down their closure plans. The development of Regional Secure Units has slowed down drastically, whilst the three expensively-run English Special Hospitals all remain in tact.[13] There is also a tendency to cut voluntary-run services first when hard-nosed decisions have to be taken at local authority level. Thus one of the latest (1990/1991) paradoxes of the implementation of the government's policy, *Caring for People*, is that whilst local planning groups are busy drawing up proposals for an expanded community service, local authorities are cutting back on existing community mental health services in order to keep down poll tax levels.

Given the 'muddling through' which has tended to dominate planning by professionals in the mental health field, user participation has the potential to provide a new direction for services. The data to be discussed below may be of some help in setting an agenda or supporting innovations by users in their local efforts to influence service provision. The views of service users are described in relation to in-patient services, day hospitals/ facilities, out-patients and the voluntary sector. The aim here is to construct a picture of how users experience and view the purpose of these services. In the next chapter, the focus is on services designed around leaving hospital.

Admission to hospital

Most of the 516 survey participants had extensive experience of hospital life, with just under half of the respondents having experienced more than four periods of hospitalisation. Sixty-five per cent of the respondents identified an unbroken period in hospital of three months or more, and 37 per cent said that they had spent a total period of seven months or more in hospital. This pattern of admission suggests that these respondents were generally 'revolving door' patients: that is, people who spend most of their time outside hospital with intermittent in-patient phases.

The majority of users (73 per cent) considered that their admission to hospital was necessary at the time of their crisis. The reasons that people gave for feeling that hospitalisation was necessary were related to the need for asylum, usually as a result of a failure to cope with their everyday lives:

Could not cope with the pressure of work and family.

I felt a need to be cared for and looked after away from everyday pressures.

It was either admission or to continue killing myself.

If I hadn't been admitted to hospital at that time I would have committed suicide.

In no fit state of mind to be left unsupervised.

I was totally out of control of my life.

To get away from the house and be with other people like myself.

I felt hopeless at my parents' place. I had the faintest of faint hopes that things might be better in hospital.

Because there seemed little alternative.

These responses indicate the desperation of many of the users at the time of their admission. Although most people viewed their hospitalisation as unavoidable, this was not accompanied by an unequivocal vote of support for in-patient services. Almost half the sample considered that an alternative to what was on offer should have been available. These included:

A humane day centre that allowed dignity.

Supervised Mother and Child home.

A stay in a residential rehabilitation hospital or unit.

User-run support system.

Centre where individual attention was available where there was some privacy.

A hostel may have been more suitable and helpful.

Alternatives were more often expressed as a personal *need* rather than as a specific form of service provision. Having someone to talk or 'relate to', alleviation of stress through holidays or being able to stay with friends were examples.

Anywhere where people would take an interest.

Being able to stay with a friend.

To be somewhere I could sleep, rest and be understood.

A long holiday involving yoga, diving and craft.

A place where people can go for a rest period and to talk about problems before it gets to the stage of going into hospital.

Being given personal attention.

Understanding and someone to care.

Keeping a job and having a flat of my own.

Help with the children.

Someone to talk to.

In contrast to the large number who wanted an alternative to hospital, only a small proportion (14.5 per cent) were ever offered another option. Moreover, these were generally quite different from the type of input that users seemed to be wanting. Where alternatives were offered the most frequent choice on offer was an out-patient appointment. Despite a number of comments suggesting that 'supervision', or visits by mental health workers to their homes, would have been preferable to hospital admission, this was rarely evident. Out of the 85 people offered an alternative to hospital, a domiciliary visit by a mental health professional was only offered in 13 instances. This indicates that services and professionals are not orientated to providing community acute care in any significant way. It also points to the paucity of alternative forms of crisis intervention apart from hospital-centred models.

Where people felt that admission was *unnecessary* at the time of their admission this was invariably related to the perceived ineffectiveness of hospitalisation.

I was crying non-stop and was put to sleep but I don't feel that it was of any help.

If I had some counselling I would have got through without hospital admission. They did not do it in them days.

I still had the same problems when I came out.

Take a long time to cure you − if at all.

Waste of time − because I don't feel they helped me. They just kept me there, [I] did not gain anything from admission.

People's experience of their hospital stay

The need for some sort of haven at times of crisis was evident in the positive comments made about hospital.[14] The aspect that respondents seemed to value the most was the security they derived in terms of asylum from the outside world, as indicated by these respondents.

> Felt secure in hospital. Began to understand my illness and felt I was being helped on the road to recovery.

> By being in hospital, it took pressure off my parents and my own family, and enabled the doctors to observe and see what treatment I needed.

> I think what a smashing place it was – the grounds; somewhere to go for a bit of peace and quiet, to recharge batteries.

> To me it was true asylum.

> It wasn't like I thought it would be. I was afraid on my way in, I thought I would be locked up. On my second visit I felt I needed to be in hospital for my own peace of mind.

Such positive comments were the exception rather than the rule.[15] Those making comments about their stay were overwhelmingly negative in their evaluations, for the reasons examined below.

Failed expectations

A clash between people's expectations and what was on offer once inside appeared to be at the root of many grievances. In particular, the ethos and approach adopted by the hospital regime (which centred on an illness model aimed primarily at the treatment of the object of illness) were offensive. Users were far more likely to view their distress in subjective terms, and the appropriate response to it as working through or talking through their problems with someone ready to listen in a supportive and caring environment. Here are some examples which highlight the gap between the positions:

I did not realise I was talking to a psychiatrist for 30 minutes into our first session – he had not introduced himself. He looked scruffy. I thought he was the cleaner. I was treated as an object – my symptoms were discussed over my head as if I wasn't there.

Although I knew I needed help I didn't receive the help I needed. Nurses didn't want to talk (something you needed desperately). Forced to help in kitchen and canteen. Forced to play silly games hardly ever seeing psychiatrists.

I felt isolated and felt there was a lack of communication. I had assumed I would be able to talk about my problems with staff.

I felt that I was in hospital to be studied and not understood.

I felt very much alone and frightened. The medical profession did not seem to realise how bad I felt and could not cope with it. There was no real communication as to MY NEEDS.

I feel I should have been given long-term psychotherapy help, counselling in which the abominations in my childhood would have been discovered. Instead I was given ECT against my wishes which I found inhumane.

I wish they listened more carefully and didn't give so much outdated treatment as a blanket cure for so many problems.

I hated hospital life – it made me crack up even more. People didn't seem to care, or maybe I didn't co-operate. Very few doctors tell you what's wrong.

Some of them wanted to be quite helpful but they didn't know how to help me – they just know how to give pills and ECT, which wasn't helpful.

Loss of citizenship

The power of the hospitals' staff and regime to take away users' status in the outside world was also a factor deeply resented. On entering the hospital, people lost the right to define themselves in the way they were used to outside. Aspects of the 'degradation ceremony', whereby people lose many of their taken-for-granted civil liberties and rights on entering hospital (as described by Goffman in 1961)[16] are still pertinent today:

> Whilst still a student but married, the clerk insisted on defining my status as 'housewife' and not 'student'.

> I didn't like having my personal belongings taken away.

> The hospital did not look after me properly when I was admitted. I lost very important personal property (certificates, books, poetry and clothes) which were taken from me. This is like state theft. If your liberty is going to be taken from you, you should be entitled to a trial in court.

Discrimination and humiliation

Discrepancies in how users were treated according to their social status and class was something that was occasionally mentioned. For example, one woman noticed how she received 'worse treatment as a Woolworth's assistant than as a student'. Whilst the way in which people were treated whilst in hospital might have varied according to social status, it seems that a loss of dignity and failure to respect the wishes or rights of individual patients is something that is experienced more generally as an in-patient on a psychiatric ward.

> I was humiliated, treated like a small child. Not enough attention was paid to people who lost articles in the hospital. It would have been more helpful if the psychiatrists had discussed my illness with me.

> The most terrible experience of my life. We were locked in the ward and kept in our nightclothes. At that time (12 years ago) I found staff unfriendly and not helpful.

> Nurses shouldn't make you strip naked to have a wash.

Depressing environment

The lack of care and empathy on the part of some of the staff was compounded frequently by a bleak and depressing environment ('the dirty and rundown state of hospital made me worse').

Coercion and brutality

A menacing aspect of patients' experience was the forced nature of treatments, the brutality personally experienced or witnessed, or just the fear that such things might occur.[17]

> I was very scared when I was put on a section; I thought they were going to beat me up.

> Had brain operation without my consenting to it.

> I'd like to say that it is unfair to lock people up without telling them why. I was extremely devastated at the time.

> It was all right if you kept quiet, otherwise they drugged you up.

From the data available, it is not possible to identify accurately the extent to which the experience of these five categories of complaint are currently prevalent. It may well have been that some of the incidents which were mentioned occurred some time ago. Nonetheless many of these incidents were described by young patients, and a sizeable proportion of the sample had been in hospital over the previous 12 months.[18] It may be reasonable to assume that they are still endemic within contemporary mental health provision. Not only have there been few old Victorian hospitals actually closed, but the mode and delivery of services has, in the main, remained the same where it is provided on other hospital sites.[19]

Thus, whilst the opportunity for abuse in DGH psychiatric units might well be less, since they are not so geographically isolated, the type of objectification and dehumanising physical treatments complained about still predominate. Moreover, paradoxically, the placement of such units in organisations designed for those with *physical* ailments makes them prone to developing new forms of restrictive and oppressive practices. For example, the need to contain distressed and distressing behaviour within a highly restricted space, and preserve order near operating theatres and other wards, might make compulsion and the restricting of psychiatric patients' movements even more commonplace. Such issues are rarely highlighted in discussions about moving from the old asylum system to DGH sites.

Discussion of findings on in-patient care

The picture painted above of patients' experiences of hospital in-patients provision is, overall, a bleak one. The majority of people felt trapped in a Catch-22 situation. Most people wanted help, or recognised in retrospect that they could not continue without some sort of intervention when they had reached a crisis point. However, rather than this need being met in an empathic, effective way most people seem to think that hospitalisation did little to ameliorate their underlying problems. In many instances it compounded them.

Whilst one interpretation of these accounts may be that a person's mental state might have affected the way in which their experience of hospitalisation has been viewed, it is unlikely that this would account for the overwhelmingly negative view of hospital admission. Many of the items identified by users, such as the objectification inherent in a medical model of mental illness, have been documented and commented upon by critics of traditional psychiatry for many years. Reports from the Health Advisory Service, Mental Health Act Commission and government inquiries also highlight many of the aspects vividly expressed here by the recipients of hospital services. All the accounts do here is confirm what has already been said before. However, one important addition is the inescapable conclusion that in-patient services — supposedly designed in the interests of patients — have, according to the judgements of these patients, failed them abysmally.

Out-patient services

Despite the criticisms made of out-patients, comparing the content of comments, they are preferred to in-patient services. Most people in the survey (85 per cent) had attended out-patients either before or subsequent to their admission to hospital. People were usually out-patients for considerable periods of time. Sixty per cent spent periods of more than a year attending out-patients, with 36 per cent attending for periods of three years or more. Table 4.1 shows ratings of the helpfulness of such attendances.

Table 4.1   Helpfulness of out-patients' attendances

Category	%
Helpful	54
Neutral	25
Unhelpful	21

$N = 427$

Main complaints about out-patient services

Poor accessibility

Accessibility to out-patient services was difficult for a quarter of those attending. One respondent reported having to travel 30 miles.

Long waits

The largest complaint on the part of users appeared to relate to excessively long waits once at the hospital. It seems that rarely was the organisation of out-patient appointments designed to meet the needs of clients (implying that professional or organisational needs were being prioritised).

Often you have to wait for long periods of time after your appointment time.

I have had over 100 appointments and 98% of them have been later than the time I was given. I am not happy about this; I now walk out if I wait too long and make a complaint to the hospital management.

You get tense waiting.

Long period of waiting followed by short time of seeing person.

Waiting time too long – three to four hours which is a psychological strain in itself.

When one is severely depressed the wait seems interminable. By the time one is with the psychiatrist often one then wishes to say very little, so that the visit is not as beneficial as it could be.

Short interviews

For many the long wait was not worth while if it was followed by a cursory interview.

> Quarter of an hour once a fortnight did nothing to help me at all. They are a waste of time and never once were any problems I had or wanted help with discussed.

> They go over the same thing. Probably useful for their assessment but not helpful to me.

> Gone away feeling worse that when I went. Condition never explained.

> Sometimes I get the impression that the person who sees me asks 'stock' questions and uses very little imagination.

> Very brief; no in-depth discussion.

Inconsistent medical staffing

The lack of consistency of medical staffing was another aspect that could be disconcerting. Although occasionally this meant that users were able to change from one psychiatrist with whom they were dissatisfied to one whom they felt that was better, a number of respondents felt that repeated changes in staffing was a negative aspect of out-patient attendance. Certainly, appointments did not conform to the notion of one practitioner building up a one-to-one relationship with a person over time. This implies the absence of a notion of a confiding affiliation in psychiatrists' meetings with their clients that we are acculturated to expect.

> Different doctors at different times, so they don't really know your case history.

> Doctors keep changing: get sick of seeing different ones.

> I have found out-patients appointments where you see different person each time worse than useless. Find them more helpful where one can see the same person, especially if they're knowledgeable about me.

> It would be better if you saw the same doctor all the time as they have to ask the same questions and it would be preferable to have a steady relationship built up with one doctor.

Positive views of out-patient services

The positive aspects of attendance identified by users were varied. Some viewed the utility of the service in preventative terms: 'Can talk about medication and side effects of medication. It's best to attend my appointments, as it can keep me out of hospital.' Access to psychiatrists that people were unable to obtain elsewhere was another thing appreciated about out-patients departments: 'It's the only time you can talk with your psychiatrists. When you are in hospital you can't see one.' Other positive aspects noted were the link between hospital and community, the chance to reassess medication regimes and the opportunity to talk over their problems.

Day facilities: hospital or community services?

Of the 516 people responding to the survey, 345 people (67 per cent) had made use of day facilities at some time. Half of this group had attended more than one facility. Arguments for retaining hospital-based acute services are often shored up by the rationale of the need to be close to medical facilities for diagnostic and other purposes. Whatever the merits and shortcomings of this point of view, it seems inappropriate to extend it to day services.

Day facilities should be the easiest type of service to locate in local community settings. By definition, people who use them are not distressed enough to be kept in hospital. However one of the most surprising results of the survey is the apparent failure to provide day facilities for people on *non-hospital* sites. Fifty-seven per cent of the last day hospitals or facilities used by respondents were located on hospital sites. This percentage was made up of 33 per cent located within psychiatric hospitals and 24 per cent on DGH sites.

The fact that such a large percentage were located on DGH sites suggests that new day facilities are not being provided by statutory agencies as far as possible in community settings. Rather, the results tend to provide evidence of the process of 'trans-hospitalisation' discussed ealier.

Problems for users of day centres still being hospital-linked

Location, it seems, was very important to users in terms of the type of service provided. In theory, being on a hospital site might not mean a traditional hospital-type service. Yet this was not how the users in our survey experienced it. Many comments seemed to suggest that the location was reflected in the environment and service delivery.

Continued institutionalised practices

An extension of the hospital ward and regimen was much in evidence, as indicated by the following respondents:

> Too many people stayed in the day hospital too long – there was no encouragement to move on.

> It should only be attended short term, because there's a danger of becoming institutionalised.

> The regimentation of it was what I liked the least.

> Dislike Radio 1 blaring out all day and depressing surroundings.

> Very medicalised and patronising.

Lack of meaningful activity

> Long stretches with little activity bore a resemblance to the lethargy and institutionalised feel of back-wards.

> I least like the sitting around and lack of contact with nurses and psychiatrists.

> Often hang around a lot with nothing to do.

A continued sense of coercion

Non-voluntary activities were another feature frequently referred to in a negative light and extended from hospital wards to day hospitals.

> Continued with patronising attitude. Had to be seen to be doing something however boring it was. When I attended the day hospital I had no choice in the matter. I was in X under Section 3 of the Mental Health Act. I kept begging the psychiatrist to let me go home as I couldn't bear it in there. Eventually I was released on condition that I attended. I did not like the fact that you had to attend OT whether

you liked it or not and getting treated like children. The only good thing was I had to get out of bed to attend.

Should be at more liberty to come and go and more scope for what you want to do.

I liked least the nagging about injections.

Didn't like the nurse's instructions.

The worst thing were the discussion groups which I was forced to attend.

However, this dislike of regimentation and medicalisation also has to be seen in the context of the most valued aspect of day services. Day facilities were regarded as slightly better than hospital admission because of their distance, albeit relative, from in-patient services.

It kept some people from the worse fate of being an inpatient — it meant you could keep up links with home.

I found the day hospital very helpful as you can spend the best part of your day and night in your home environment.

Problems of accessibility

The question of accessibility to day service facilities is perhaps more important than in relation to other services. Not only do people have to find their way to and from such provision every day, but many people use this facility over extensive periods of time. In this survey 41 per cent had attendance rates of more than one year, with just under one-fifth (19) attending for periods of more than three years. If one of the objectives of day facilities is to widen or promote the social networks of clients, then this has to be done with an eye to where people live. It should also help users build on the social contact they make with others attending services.

Respondents were asked how accessible they found the day facility they were attending by foot or public transport. A quarter found access difficult or very difficult. Some people identified this as the worst aspect of attending day services.

It was a long way to go for a short period.

The journey was the worst part because I had to catch two buses.

In some instances this lack of accessibility prevented people from continuing to use the service. There are, of course, other reasons for why clients might find it difficult to attend day facilities: for example, it may be due to some physical disability necessitating an ambulance service. Whilst the use of this form of transport might be unavoidable in some instances, comments seem to suggest that overall this was not a favoured option. Possibly this was because of the connotations of using a hospital rather than a community service. Geographical isolation was not the only way in which users defined the accessibility of the service. Lack of child care facilities was also a barrier to attendance: one user said, 'No help was offered with baby care. Experienced severe difficulties with minders whilst attending.'

Inflexibility of opening times

Attention was also drawn to the rigidity of the times people could use the centres. Most seemed to operate on a 9–5 weekday routine. Whilst this may be more convenient to the staff working in such facilities, it did not seem to meet the needs of many of the respondents.

What I liked least was they only open office hours and closed at weekends.

I would have liked it to stay open till 6.00 instead of 4.30.

There could be more social clubs in the evenings.

The worst thing is the lack of evening facilities.

Although I made friends in hospital I lost friends at home. I found the evenings and week-ends very lonely.

The benefits of day care

The above demand for greater flexibility is more understandable when the most valued aspects of day provision are examined. It seems that the social links and company of other users are the things most highly regarded. Overall, respondents found attending day facilities beneficial. Forty-five per cent rated the service as helpful whilst 11 per cent found them unhelpful. The remainder adopted an indifferent stance towards their attendance. Whilst a 45 per cent satisfaction rate is hardly a glowing endorsement, it reflects better on services than the views expressed about hospital admissions.

When examining the more specific aspects of what is on offer at day centres (see Figure 4.1), a mixed picture emerges as to the benefits of attending day care facilities.

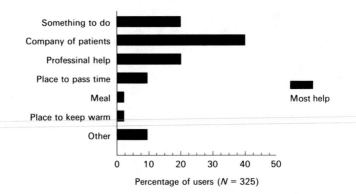

Figure 4.1 Perceived usefulness of day services

Human contact

The largest group of respondents identified the 'company of other patients' as the most helpful aspect of day services.

> The things I enjoyed most about the day hospital was meeting people in general and having facilities whereby I could use my hands.

> Local day centre was valuable for giving something to do and meeting people.

> The company kept me going.

> It helped me to get away from the house environment situation. I have the opportunity to make friends.

The day centre offers company; we all help each other.

Basically I think it's a good idea to attend a day centre, I've made new friends.

The best thing is the encouragement of other patients.

The best thing was the friends I had and the least was losing them when I was discharged.

I enjoy attending to meet other people, takes my mind off worrying about my nerves.

Occasionally, other patients were not seen as a positive feature of attending day services. For example:

I didn't like being with the old people, it made me think that I would end up like them, i.e. very confused and demented.

Felt like there was too much of a mixture of problems with patients attending ranging from serious to not so serious.

Mixing with older and more ill patients I found depressing.

Some patients were rather frightening.

Useful activities

Practical activities, such as needlework and carpentry, were often appreciated. Activities which had long term pay-offs in other ways were particularly highly valued. One patient said, 'It was very helpful to learn how to use computers. I'm now secretary in a local organisation – found this job through the day facility.' Although, overall, activities were viewed positively there were also a number of strongly expressed negative comments about activities.

Useless, non-productive, utterly boring and childish.

I only stayed for two days because the patients were being whipped up into hysteria by playing silly games. This was not stimulating for me. I was bored. No choice.

Resented going because it was tedious. Art available at a level for 6 year olds, i.e. cutting out shapes, etc.

No structured programme or approach – offered very little apart from kindergarten stuff.

Ambivalence towards therapy

There seemed to be a marked distinction between those wanting therapeutic intervention and those wanting to use day facilities for making social contacts. Some seemed to not find the 'activities', such as games, art and discussion groups, helpful. Instead they valued psychological therapies highly and thought they would benefit from more of this type of intervention.

Learning how to relax was very helpful (with tapes). Also I had a very helpful course in cognitive therapy from a psychiatrist.

Dislike washing up for 30 people.

Should be more group therapy – the most helpful thing. Should explore all possibilities of helping patients, including spiritual healing.

However, that such a high rate of people attended for the company of others, and something to do, indicates a general preference for social interaction as opposed to distinct forms of 'therapy'. This was also indicated by some of the comments made by respondents.

Attended a group therapy session for depressives which was unhelpful.

The art activities were of extreme value, but I did not get on with my one-to-one sessions with staff which led to difficulties.

Best liked the drama and least liked the psychotherapy.

Comments on day services indicated that people clearly had differing expectations as to what day services ought to provide. The term 'therapy' can encompass anything from cooking to psychoanalysis as far as mental health professionals are concerned.

Ordinary activities, if deemed to be helpful, become 'therapeutic' in their eyes. However, users themselves distinguish between activities, such as cooking, drama or art (even if presented in the guise of therapy), and psychological interventions. Thus distinctions were made, for example, between group therapy and general discussion groups. This distinction made by users suggests the need for a clearer philosophy on the part of those providing services as to the purpose and rationale of varying activities and interventions. Perhaps this would lead to a recognition of the need for a diverse range of services and activities. If separated conceptually by providers they might meet varying needs more efficiently. Currently it is commonly assumed that every psychiatric patient requires a similar type of service and can be catered for under one roof. A further indication of the need to tailor services to differing groups of patient was an awareness on the part of respondents of the different 'types' of patient using day services. The issue of mixing those with degenerative neurological disorders, such as dementia, was mentioned above. Others were aware of differing levels of distress.

> The worst part was being on the day ward with very ill patients – very depressing.

> Didn't like the fact that the groups were mixed having people with severe and less serious problems together.

> Felt they were for people less fortunate than me – 'subnormal people'.

Others rejected both the activities and therapy, preferring normalised options. A few respondents said they never used day services for long because what they wanted was real employment and this was the priority for them when getting over a crisis. Some felt that professionals ought to spend more time putting people in touch with outside social and economic opportunities. In this respect, users can be seen to be more intuitively in touch with the findings of research that show the benefits of such options for recovering from mental health problems:

> A lot of time was spent playing silly games. Would have been much better getting assistance to join clubs, societies outside of hospital and mixing with people who were not ill.

They need a more realistic attitude toward getting back to work, to stop the decline into being dependent on the day unit. One gets into a rut and they should be trying to help us bridge the gap between being ill and getting back to work.

I wish I didn't need to go. I want a job.

Would prefer to be in employment.

The best part was the practical help, and information about mental illness.

Are day service staff useful?

Indirectly, the positive role of the staff is reflected in the provision of activities which are considered useful by users of day facilities. Also, overall, staff *were* considered to be helpful far more often than their hospital counterparts. However, one of the reasons that professional help was not more frequently seen as the most useful aspect of attending day services (see Figure 4.1) was because of them being unable to help towards meeting external, social, long-term goals. That is, the priorities of the users were not always those of the staff. Another reason for the fairly low ratings given to staff, compared to other aspects of day care provision, was the attitude that staff adopted towards patients. One aspect, which was particularly noted, was the patronising and authoritarian manner of staff.

Often staff were unhelpful with comments like 'you are not listening, you are going round in circles'.

What I liked least was the rigid attitudes and close mindedness of the majority of the occupational therapists.

I found the staff to be patronising.

Attitudes of staff need changing to clients — from indifference to encouragement and to look at reality from the patient's view.

Mystification was something which also tended to be viewed negatively: 'The two workers use jargon and this I dislike the most. This is also a power thing as well.' In these instances there is a lack of awareness that users *are* offended by being treated like children, and that authoritarianism and rigidity is not greatly appreciated. When this is true, it is because staff, not patients, are out of touch with reality and lack insight. Users seem to be asking for more equitable and co-operative relationships in which their adulthood is recognised and endorsed.

The criticisms of staff, together with a desire on the part of respondents for greater choice and user participation, suggests the need for a new model of working between those using day services and those providing it.

Impact of cuts in day services

A final comment that needs recording about the users' accounts of day services concerns cut-backs in provision. This was not in evidence in the other responses about services. Cuts in resources in this area seem completely at odds with the ostensible prioritising of non-in-patient services.

> The facilities were good – all the daily papers, library, snooker table, etc. These services have now been drastically reduced.

> Going to fold due to lack of resources and I think it should continue. Offices are expanding whilst actual activities are being reduced.

> Although I gained benefit from it, it has now been seriously cut back.

Views of the voluntary sector

One significant complement (but also counter-current) to the present state-run mental health services is the voluntary sector. Agencies, such as MIND and the Richmond Fellowship, have developed a network of residential and non-residential services to respond to the material and personal needs of clients. The users in this survey were asked their views about their involvement with voluntary groups and to compare their experience with state-delivered professional services. Not surprisingly, given that the sample was drawn mostly from MIND associations, comments related to users' experience of local MIND groups. This, of course, might have created a positive bias in the material in favour of

MIND groups. However, most respondents were able to identify very *specific* aspects of their contact with voluntary organisations rather than make all-embracing statements ('Very good', etc.), which suggests that these were valid responses rather than biased artefacts.

Overall, users tended to be more positive about the voluntary sector than they were about statutory services.

> Attended group at MIND day centre. Found people working for MIND helpful and more informative than professionals. Treated as an equal and not inferior.

> Regularly attended MIND drop-in. Feel more relaxed there than at hospital or social services day centre. Also information about drugs is readily available.

> Attend MIND day centre – contact less disciplined, more like a family situation than health centre. More informal and prefer it to professional services, find it more enjoyable.

> I find I am able to speak on a one-to-one basis without having to wait. I would rather go to MIND than hospital.

> Felt had gained nothing from professional services. From MIND, gained ability to face and cope with anxiety in day-to-day life.

> I spent 18 months at the MIND day centre after my stay in hospital and it helped me to return to a more normal way of life. We all worked and socialised together; it was a happy time and nothing like being a patient.

What are the lessons from and about the voluntary sector?

These examples seem to suggest that informality, helpfulness and being treated as equals are appreciated in voluntary provision. Services and sources of help that people found, which were not available in the state-run sector, included a number of non-traditional types of intervention. These were predominantly of a social or material sort, and included tranquilliser withdrawal groups, telephone help lines, 'drop-in centres', self-help groups and help with accommodation.

Whilst it is the case that the voluntary sector often acts to plug the gaps of the statutory sector, the data suggests that the network of voluntary organisations are also presenting *alternatives* to the latter. For example, major tranquilliser withdrawal support groups are not typically available in NHS mental health services because they run counter to the dominant treatment philosophy of treatment by psychotropic drugs. Such groups would inevitably threaten medical interventions by acknowledging openly the iatrogenic effects of tranquillisers. They might even be seen to encourage 'non-compliance' amongst patients.

Mutuality and support facilitated by the less formal structure of the voluntary sector were also features that users found helpful and lacking in statutory services. Thus, in this context, deprofessionalisation and deskilling (the erosion of specialist skills held by professionals) are seen as positive by users. This ethos directly clashes with that of professionals, who favour professionalisation strategies (such as lengthy formal training and the acquisition of specialist skills).

In the statutory sector, professional boundaries prevent participation by users in the delivery of services. These barriers are less evident in the voluntary sector. Having a useful social role in the actual delivery of services was something that was highly valued and not available as an opportunity from the statutory sector. It seems that to be merely passive recipients of care or therapy is not enough but that active engagement in collectively providing and promoting services is also something that users highly value in recovery from distress and participating in local community life.

I used to be very involved with the MIND day centre and we did lots of activities. It kept me occupied and I used to help out as a volunteer. It helped me to settle back into the community.

I have been voted chairman of the local MIND group.

Started self-help group with six others, have found this very useful.

Got involved in volunteering and this helped me to begin leading a normal life and I am now working full time in the voluntary sector.

However, it was evident that this was sometimes limited by the structural, dependent position of MIND to its state funders as illustrated by this response: 'Approached local MIND re complaining about treatment at local unit. Given very little help — told that they were aware of situation but were afraid to interfere lest they were deprived of their grant from the local authority.'

Overall, users identified a preference for the informal social support provided by the voluntary sector. This was compared favourably with the formal, costly, professionally-dominated services provided by the state sector. Given the preference for such forms of service, it is noteworthy that the current proportion of the mental health service budget supporting the voluntary sector is insignificant when compared to the budget available to the statutory services.[20]

Of course, one of the reasons that the state-run services can claim a greater slice of the funding cake is because of their social control function (their mandate under the Mental Health Act to lock people up). Another argument, which might be put forward in defence of statutory provision, is that acute mental health crises require heavy staffing levels. These crises are not dealt with by the voluntary sector. Whilst this is undoubtedly the case at present, there is no reason why such services have to remain exclusively inside the statutory sector. Although exceptional, there are models of good practice already in existence in the voluntary sector (such as, the Arbours Association), suggesting that it is possible to provide credible acute services outside the state-run sector. Moreover, there are growing demands for alternative acute services from user groups (such as 24-hour community-based crisis intervention teams, crisis houses and temporary user-run asylums) because state provision is seen as too hospital based, inflexible and oppressive.

One of the main reasons that the voluntary sector has remained under-funded and under-utilised is because of the negative rather than positive way in which it has been conceptualised politically. Many Labour-run local authorities have failed to support the voluntary sector because of an assumption that state-run services are, *ipso facto*, superior and should be prioritised, and that the voluntary sector provides non-essential, amateurish services. Furthermore, organised unionised work forces carry greater weight with their direct authority employers than their more distant counterparts in the voluntary sector. There has also been a mistaken tendency to equate voluntary sector provision with privately-run for-profit services, which do not find favour with Labour authorities. Thus, under resource constraints, it is not unusual for voluntary projects to be the first to have their funding cut, even when local authority funding for mental health services is small. Conservative philosophy has over the last decade been more supportive of the notion of providing a more robust voluntary sector. The role envisaged for the voluntary sector in the new government proposals for community care outlined in *Caring for People* is evidence of this. However, the role is one which conceives the voluntary sector as *replacing* existing state services. This runs counter to the ethos of the more progressive elements in the voluntary sector. An example of this can be seen in the 1988 Social Security Act, which abolished grants and introduced loans for household goods. Voluntary organisations were cajoled into plugging the gap left by the withdrawal of essential items for subsistence, and ended up providing items such as furniture and clothing.

Moreover, the present government policy of involving the voluntary sector more fully, in its plans for community care has not taken into account the weaker structural position of the voluntary sector in relation to the planning and provision of services. For example, the voluntary sector cannot realistically compete with Trust-run services if the latter have a monopoly over use of buildings. Neither does current government philosophy take account of the spread of voluntary sector provision, which tends to be inverse to need. There is, for example, less voluntary provision in predominantly working-class areas than more affluent ones.[21] Absorbing the limited energies of the voluntary sector into a more service-orientated role might also lead to the weakening of their traditional campaigning role in pressing for better state service provision. Thus there appear to be major structural and political barriers to providing funds for a comprehensive voluntary sector service which can compete effectively with state-run services.

Conclusion

Data presented in this chapter about hospital-run services show only limited support from those who use them. Many aspects of this provision fell well short of users' expectations and needs. This did not only include complaints of overt abuse or dehumanising treatment: a rigid medicalised service delivery which objectifies and patronises people does not seem to be much appreciated either. There was only weak evidence of the state sector being able to meet the individual needs of clients, which in general seem modest enough: someone to talk to during a crisis, a choice of activities and treatment, and adequate material and social support. In contrast to the faint praise awarded to the statutory sector, voluntary sector provision was greatly appreciated. In this respect the voluntary sector provides examples of practice which the state sector could well emulate. This applies particularly to the informal individualised response to distress, which these respondents felt was generally missing from formal services. Opportunities for participation in the running and delivery of services is another issue which the state sector could learn much about from the voluntary sector. However, it is more difficult to envisage this becoming a reality given the power of self-serving strategies entrenched in the mental health professions. Such a development would require a wholesale rejection of many of the highly valued aspects of the lengthy training received by mental health professionals. This tradition militates against professionals handing over power and responsibility to the users of services.

Notes and References

1. *Better Services for the Mentally Ill* (London: HMSO, 1977).
2. Dalley, G., *Ideologies of Caring* (London: Macmillan, 1988).
3. Sayce, L., (ed.), *Community Mental Health Centres Report of the Annual Conference 1987* (London: National Unit of Psychiatry Research and Development, 1987).
4. Health and Personal Social Services Statistics for England (London: Department of Health and Social Services, 1987); recent estimates are that psychiatric beds constitute 36% of all hospital beds (Hospital and Community Health Services Budget, House of Commons Session 1987/8).
5. There are more than 50 000 patients in psychiatric beds in England alone, at any one time: *Mental Health in the 1990s: From Custody to Care* (London: Office of Health Economics, 1989).
6. Brown, G., 'The Mental Hospital as an Institution', *Social Science and Medicine*, 7 (1973), pp. 407–24.
7. Baruch, G. and Treacher, A., *Psychiatry Observed* (London: Routledge & Kegan Paul, 1978).
8. Crepet, P. and Deplato, G., 'Psychiatry without Asylums: Origins and Prospects in Italy', *The International Journal of Health Services*, 13, 1 (1983), pp. 119–29.
9. For example, between 1977 and 1987 Community Mental Health Centres expanded from 1 to 54: Sayce, L., *Community Mental Health Centres Report*, p. 3.

10. Tomlinson, D., *Utopia, Community Care and the Retreat from the Asylums* (Milton Keynes: Open University Press, 1991).

11. Good Practices in Mental Health (a charitable organisation set up in the 1970s to identify and promote innovative practice) often picks out such services for special mention.

12. 'Society Tomorrow', 1 August 1984. Maxwell Jones interviewed by Ann Shearer, *The Guardian*.

13. Though a large increase in funding has now been promised to deal with what is now regarded as a crisis in secure provision for mentally disordered offenders: see *The Guardian*, 28 January 1992.

14. Respondents were asked in an open-ended way about their experiences of hospital: 'Looking back overall to your admissions to psychiatric hospitals what comments would you wish to make.'

15. Out of 124 comments made in response to the open question, 101 were negative.

16. Goffman, E., *Asylums* (Harmondsworth: Penguin, 1961).

17. Examples of many of these incidents have already been discussed in the previous chapter.

18. 35 per cent of the sample were aged below 35 years of age, and 37 per cent of the sample had been in hospital during 1989/1990.

19. As indicated by recent Health Advisory and Mental Health Act Commission reports: see for example, *Decay, Squalor and Neglect* (London: MIND, 1988).

20. According to one source voluntary groups receive less than 1 per cent of local authority budgets: Leat, D., 'The Role of the Voluntary Sector', in *Informal Care Tomorrow* (London: Policy Studies Institute, 1986).

21. Langan, M., 'Community Care in the 1990s: The Community Care White Paper *Caring for People*', *Critical Social Policy*, 29 (1990) pp. 58–70.

5
Views on Community Living

The last chapter dealt with mainly hospital-based services. This chapter will explore life for patients living in the community. What do service users think of GPs? What are the stresses of working? Are users helped by services to re-gain or find employment? What sort of accommodation do users want? What are the experiences users have of being unemployed and living on state benefits? The role of GPs will be examined first.

Professional and policy background to data on GPs

Recently, attention has been given to extending the role of primary health care to respond increasingly to elderly patients, people with learning difficulties and those with mental health problems. The recognition that, for most people, the health centre is their first port of call in seeking formal help, as well as being an agency that provides ongoing health surveillance, is largely responsible for GPs being identified as having a pivotal part to play in 'community care'. From quite a different source, critical attention has recently been focused on GPs as a result of a sustained campaign surrounding the over-prescribing and side-effects of minor tranquillisers.

In the mental health field, plans to expand the GPs' role have provoked an anxious concern from psychiatrists about their own professional interests. The ability of psychiatrists to maintain their dominant position within mental health is based on the credibility of their diagnostic abilities and particular knowledge of psychotropic drugs. Expanding the GPs' role in these areas inevitably threatens the continued rationale for a continued 'specialist' role for psychiatry. Academic research and debate within psychiatry have been preoccupied with the issue of whether GPs can recognise and treat 'mental illness' adequately, and to what extent they can substitute for trained psychiatrists in the area of diagnosis. When faced with encroachment from other groups, medical specialists typically will query their competitors' competence.

The increased focus on the importance of general practice in mental health has been stimulated by, and reflected in, government policy towards primary health care services. For example, the proposals in the Government's White Paper, *Promoting Better Health*[1] provides incentives for GPs to employ counsellors by lifting some of the restrictions on reimbursement of costs. Despite these incentives, it seems that many GPs have been slow to take up the option of employing counselling staff. For example, one local survey of counselling services provided by GPs in the London area showed that, in one district, only nine people were employed specifically to provide counselling.[2] The same survey showed that, although GPs supported this approach in so far as the overwhelming majority referred people elsewhere for counselling, the most common agency used was a hospital clinic. It seems that GPs still prefer to provide the main mental health service within primary health care themselves or to share it with their specialist psychiatric colleagues. In the light of this background, let us look at what our respondents said about GPs.

Views about GPs

According to our survey, GPs are the most important 'gatekeepers' as far as the first contact with the mental health services is concerned (60 per cent of people first came into contact with services via this route). They also provide considerable ongoing support and a point of contact outside hospital-based services and professionals. Sixty-three per cent of the total sample surveyed ($N = 326$) had visited their GP regarding a mental health problem within the last year. Of this group, just over half (52 per cent) can be said to have made frequent and extensive use of their GP, in that they visited on more than four occasions.

Generally there was a vote of confidence for GP services from users, especially when compared to the evaluations given to their hospital-based colleagues. There were differences in users' ratings of psychiatrists compared to GPs with regard to perceived helpfulness and attitude towards them as clients. Around 81 per cent of those who responded reported that they had generally found their family doctor to have been helpful, compared to 59 per cent of people who had reported their psychiatrist to have been helpful. Similarly, whereas 62.5 per cent of respondents considered their GP adopted a positive attitude towards them, only 45 per cent of people said they thought psychiatrists had such an attitude. Thus, overall, users preferred their GPs to their psychiatrists.

What do users like about GPs?

There were two broad types of vote of confidence in GPs: the ordinary, not 'specialised', relationship, and the 'fix-it' role. With the former, in addition to respect, kindness and availability, further grounds on which GPs were deemed by some to be helpful related, paradoxically perhaps, to the fact that they were *not* part of mainstream mental health services: that is, their distance from hospital-based psychiatry was positively rather than negatively valued by users. This contrasts with the view of psychiatrists that the GPs' lack of knowledge about 'mental illness' disadvantages patients. Such a concern seems to affect psychiatrists but not their patients. Examples of the avoidance of orthodox services are illustrated by the following responses:

As friendly and helpful as a professional relationship will allow. My GP does his best to keep me out of hospital.

Open-minded and sympathetic even though he doesn't know much about the problems themselves, and I don't expect him to.

My GP has always been very understanding but sometimes in the past I think he has been worried about whether I have received the right psychiatric treatment. I don't think he has much confidence in the consultant psychiatrist in this area and neither have I.

He has been quite positive. I asked him if I could see my report from my psychiatrist and he let me read them. This feels good.

I think she's marvellous. She doesn't condemn or regard me as neurotic — which sometimes I wonder if I'm being — she always checks to see that I'm medically well or follows through problems that I present.

He discusses alternatives to drug therapy. Is keen on exercise and 'natural' ways of living. Lets me go at my own pace.

In contrast to this dominant view, a few users viewed the non-hospital orientation of GPs in a different light, preferring to discuss their mental health problem with specialist workers. This was apparently also the view of some of the GPs, who preferred to maintain a division of labour which allowed psychiatry to deal with this aspect of their patients' lives, as indicated by some of the quotes below:

I don't tell my GP everything. I usually talk with my psychiatrist and social worker.

He [the GP] makes it clear that he prefers me to see a psychiatrist if there are problems.

Dispenses medication but psychiatrist deals with mental health problems.

It is not a GP's specialisation so he refers to a psychiatrist.

My GP only acts on the instructions passed on to him by the consultant at the hospital.

As regards the 'fix-it' role, according to a number of the responses GPs are also of considerable use because of their liaison function and ability to secure social resources.

Helped me get into a MIND hostel by writing a report. Arranged for me to see a psychiatrist at Central Middlesex. Helpful in writing medical certificates for invalidity benefits even though I have to cope with his nasty attitude.

He liaises with the hospital so everybody knows what's going on. If he's worried about me he comes to see me and if I'm worried, I contact him.

Continues to give me sick notes which is helpful for claiming benefit.

What do GPs do which is unhelpful?

Of those who regarded their GPs as being *unhelpful* a number of themes emerged.

Insufficient contact time

This echoes the problem of cursory consideration by doctors in out-patient services:

> Doesn't listen; he is too brief, he can't spend enough time with me.

The treatment of those experiencing distress needs time and sensitivity. GPs appear to have neither.

> He's very nice and sympathetic, but doesn't have the time to really understand.

Poor physical care

It was apparent that people's physical problems were sometimes dismissed or not taken seriously because of their status as psychiatric patients.

> He probably thinks I am a bit of a hypochondriac and when referred for a medical condition wrote a letter minimising a very serious condition.

> Because I have been labelled mentally ill GPs have treated me as just that. Not taking anything I say seriously and just generally trying to get me out of the surgery as quickly as possible.

> Difficulty in getting full regular medical check-up as every symptom considered as a sign of stress.

Alternatives not offered

Another negative evaluation was the failure of some GPs to consider forms of treatment other than drugs. A particular complaint was the doctor's antipathy towards 'talking' instead of prescribing.

> Sometimes I feel that a chat with my GP would have been better than increasing my medication.

Doctor never says anything, has just given repeat prescriptions since 1954.

He does not seem to understand about feelings or the way I am feeling. He only seems able to help if a tablet will do. I do not feel confident that he will listen.

Her attitude is that I need to stay on medication, otherwise I will become ill again.

They seem to think that the drugs they give are not addictive but they are.

Too inclined towards heavy medication.

He's simply a 'pusher', and I love him for his honesty in that.

He refused my request for counselling without giving reasons why.

He gave me too much Largactil. He got in trouble. It's no good. I had to go into hospital because of it.

I regret not questioning the repeat prescriptions for tranquillisers and sleeping tablets for seven years. I would probably still be on them if I had not taken myself off them.

Despite this general trend towards 'pill pushing', as reported by respondents, there were GPs who adopted more sensitive and flexible policies in relation to the prescribing of drugs:

Did give me anti-depressants which I did not find effective. Doctor accepted this and withdrew them.

He's excellent — it was good that he encouraged me to come off tranquillisers.

GP has helped by talking and listening.

He is concerned that I should not relapse but wishes to reduce medication. I find his attitude cooperative and more helpful than in the past.

Insufficient information on side-effects of drugs

As medical practitioners, GPs were primarily concerned with the benefits of drugs to control the 'symptoms' of 'mental illness'. The patients were far more interested in the side-effects and making informed decisions about the pros and cons of taking medication. This viewpoint was illustrated in a number of comments made:

> He thinks I'm a bit of a damned nuisance. I became addicted to Ativan — he didn't think this was a problem.

> Initially not enough information given. Now I'm addicted to three sets of tablets because I wasn't told.

> He thinks I'm neurotic, especially as I refuse to take any drugs he suggests. I think he now realises it was not what I needed and he can see I am now free of my distress and leading a normal life.

> They seem to think that the drugs they give are not addictive but they are.

Although there were high rates of dissatisfaction with the amount of information provided, in comparative terms the proportion of those complaining about these aspects in their contact with GPs was smaller than in relation to psychiatrists. Fifty-two per cent of respondents considered that GPs did not explain their condition in sufficient detail, compared to 75 per cent of psychiatrists. Twenty-seven per cent of people thought that information provided about treatment was inadequate from GPs, compared to the majority who thought psychiatrists failed in this respect.

Lessons for GPs from the data

From the above description of the way in which users perceived their contact with their family doctors, it seems that GPs are in an appropriate position to provide an important support role for people with mental health problems living in the community. However, paternalism, demonstrated by the limited disclosure of information and few alternatives to medication, seems to be an impediment to building a trustworthy and appreciated relationship with users.

The vital role of employment

Out of all the debates on community mental health care delivery, the issue of finding employment and improving the employment rights of ex-patients has the lowest profile. The professional literature and planning discussions at local level tend to focus on such themes as: the 'problems' of providing mental health care; interdisciplinary working in the community; and administrative barriers to the implementation of hospital run-down programmes.[3] Little mention is made of employment opportunities (or, more appropriately, the lack of them). Yet there is increasing evidence that employment is crucially important in enabling people to recover from mental health problems and the role of being a psychiatric patient.

Warner,[4] one of the few psychiatrists to show an interest in the employment status of those diagnosed as mentally ill, has summarised the research literature on the availability of employment and its impact on mental health. Research, conducted mainly in the three decades of labour scarcity after the Second World War, suggests a relationship between increased mental health problems, economic decline and depressed work opportunities. Higher recovery or discharge rates are noted in times of full employment, suggesting that when there is a need for people to do the work, ex-patients can fulfil this role as adequately as anyone else. However, a major methodological problem with this type of research is that it can only very generally trace the effect of 'down-turns' in the economy and their impact on crude indicators of mental health, such as admission to mental hospitals. Far less is known about the effects of employment and unemployment on an individual's mental health as opposed to statistical groupings of populations. The responses from our survey shed some light on the relationship between work and the experience of mental health problems for users.

Work-related problems

When asked to describe the type of problems which led to contact with the mental health services, 9 per cent of the 516 respondents identified 'work stress' or some other aspect of their employment as the primary factor leading to a crisis. Nearly three times as many men reported this to be the case as women. A proportion of this discrepancy may be linked to the slightly higher rate of employment for men compared to women before the onset of mental health problems,[5] but it may also be linked to the greater importance that work has culturally had for men (see Chapter 2). The pressures associated with changing jobs also appeared to contribute to problems. This point is illustrated by the experience of these two men.

Suffered from depression, suicidal thoughts and anxiety following exhaustion and strain caused by taking up a new job; moving away from an old job and place that I'd got used to; adapting to new circumstances, people and locality. I missed what I'd left behind and was faced with moral and personality problems at the new job. There were problems with the job itself which was demanding intellectually and emotionally.

I decided to give up my job as a miner to enrol with the National Sea Training School. Problems occurred when I discovered I couldn't cope with the rigid training. I became more and more depressed with the situation which eventually led to my breakdown. I had made the wrong choice for my future – I took on more than I was capable of, for example managing several different tasks (waiting on tables, tying knots, rowing and life saving coupled with physical exercises).

It was rare for respondents to identify work alone as responsible for the onset of a problem. Other pressing factors were also implicated. In one instance, a woman said she experienced her first 'psychotic' episode at work, but it was also apparent that the immediate employment context was by no means solely responsible. Away from home at the time she was also experiencing: 'a family breakdown back in England, highly stressful experiences in Paris during the riots of 1968 (e.g. being knocked unconscious by the police). I was also raped at this time in my life.' Another woman went back to work not having fully recovered physically from an attack of typhoid, and found that on top of this 'the stress of work was too much'.

The stress of unemployment

Only 10 people mentioned unemployment as a principal cause of problems which led them into contact with the mental health services (8 men and 2 women).[6] The reasons why unemployment was not more frequently cited as a reason, given the existing epidemiological evidence of the link between mental distress and unemployment, are not entirely clear. It may be the case that people are more likely to identify and report more immediate personal factors in the chain of events leading to distress, rather than more distant, generally social, aspects of their lives such as 'housing' or 'unemployment'. The way in which people link the experience of unemployment to mental health problems is illustrated by the following examples: 'It was being home with nothing to do. I had been unemployed for six years − I hadn't been able to work because I'd had three coronaries. Although I had an understanding wife this led to being admitted to hospital for two and half months.' Lack of social contact was apparently also a factor for this man: 'Unhappiness due to unemployment. I became mute and lived as a recluse.' Another said: 'I was on the streets roaming around looking for work, trying to fill up time. I stopped eating food, took lots of cold showers. I thought I was some kind of super hero.'

The employment prospects of psychiatric patients

There were a number of indications from the survey that employment prospects for those interviewed were severely and irreversibly damaged by entering the role of psychiatric patient. Fifty-three per cent of the sample (269 people) had a job at the time they experienced their first mental health crisis. At the time of interview, only 20 per cent of respondents reported being in any type of paid employment. Of these only 11 per cent (57 people) reported being in full-time employment, with 9 per cent having a part-time job. The impact on people's financial status was also significant, with only 16 per cent of the total sample identifying their job as providing them with their main source of income at the point when the survey was being conducted.

A number of interrelated factors seem to affect employment after a person has been in hospital. These include: the emotional residue or impact of a mental health crisis; the stigmatising and institutional effects of time spent in the psychiatric system; and discrimination by employers on learning that someone has been given the label of mental illness. The findings of a survey carried out in the mid-1980s,[7] concerning work applicants who demonstrated equal experience and training, showed that employers discriminated against those who 'confessed' to having had a mental health problem at some time in the past. It is impossible to disentangle these closely associated factors from one another in a way which could measure their relative impact on employment prospects. However, the following accounts from users give some sense of their interrelationship.

Impact of the mental health problem on work role

Sixty-three per cent of respondents said that the problem which had led to contact with the psychiatric services had affected their jobs. With regard to the availability of paid employment, 58 per cent reported their experience as having adversely affected their overall financial situation. A small number of people chose to leave their jobs as expressed by this person: 'I decided to forget the past, by working in a completely new, fresh field.' However, a more common situation was an enforced direct loss of employment:

I lost my job. I found I wasn't able to do the job I was employed for.

Took six months off sick, then I was asked to resign.

I was unable to return to paid employment.

I got suspended from work in the end until I agreed to have psychiatric treatment.

They got fed up with me having time off so I was dismissed.

Lost job due to hospital admission.

My career was effectively ended by my illness.

Just could not continue.

There were other adverse consequences, one of which was a loss of confidence at work or in seeking employment:

How I saw the future affected my chance of getting work.

I had no confidence in a work situation. Felt that other people were better than me.

I felt that people always had to help me when I worked.

Relationships with colleagues frequently deteriorated:

Staff relationships became very strained.

I couldn't speak to people a lot of the time.

Some felt they could not work to the same ability as they had prior to their crisis:

I found I was unable to do paper work.

After it happened I couldn't cope with a pressurising job.

Mixed reactions from employers

Respondents had mixed views about how employers had responded to their mental health crisis. Out of the 290 people, just under half (44.5 per cent) felt that their employers had been helpful at the time of their crisis. Just over one-third (34 per cent) considered that their employers had responded in a negative way, whilst 21 per cent rated their employers as being neither helpful nor unhelpful:

The job I had was miles from my home but they gave me support – though for convenience it would have been better to have worked nearer.

I was offered a lower-level job and salary freeze on recovery.

Does vocational training help?

In addition to labour market conditions contributing to the cause of mental health problems, there is evidence to suggest that employment opportunities are crucial to rehabilitation and overcoming the experience of a crisis. It is thought, for example, that the improved recovery rate for those diagnosed as schizophrenic in Switzerland, compared to other Western nations, is due to the favourable employment and socio-economic conditions experienced by Swiss ex-patients.[8] Recovery rates from 'schizophrenia' are also better in the non-industrial world than in Western societies. This is thought to be directly related to the ease with which people are returned to a valued working role and to more optimistic, less stigmatising cultural assumptions about recovery.[9] Given this evidence, interventions from professionals might enable users to gain or re-gain employment and thereby aid their recovery. Here we look at the data related to this proposition.

Occupational therapy

Services with a direct remit for enhancing employment skills and opportunities are, indirectly, occupational therapy (OT) and, more directly, industrial therapy (IT). The former tends to concentrate on the maintenance and development of other skills (such as cooking) and is usually part of a patient's daily routine in hospital as well as forming part of day services. The 'diversionary' function of OT is thus difficult to disentangle from its role in providing new or lost skills to patients after leaving hospital.

Three-quarters of the respondents (390 people) had attended an OT department in a psychiatric hospital or unit. In general terms, people appeared to be fairly positive towards OT (see Tables 5.1 and 5.2). Fifty-eight per cent found the activities conducted in such departments 'interesting', although this still left a substantial minority who felt the activities were either 'boring' or who were neutral in their appraisal.

Table 5.1   Evaluation of occupational therapy

Category	%
Very interesting	18.7
Interesting	39.5
Neither interesting nor boring	18.5
Boring	13.1
Very boring	10.2

$N = 390$

The most useful aspects of attending OT were felt to be the activities, the company of other people and 'somewhere to pass the time' (echoing the same priority for users of day services see Figure 5.1). Professional help was not as highly valued as might

Table 5.2   Helpfulness of occupational therapy staff

Category	%
Very helpful	34.3
Helpful	39.7
Neither helpful nor unhelpful	17.8
Unhelpful	5.6
Very unhelpful	2.6

$N = 390$

have been expected, with only 14 per cent identifying this as the most useful aspect of attendance, although it should be acknowledged that the activities arranged are in large part determined by the staff.

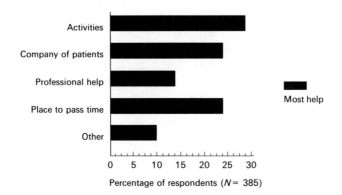

Figure 5.1 Perceived usefulness of occupational therapy

In an open-ended way, 222 people commented on OT. Their remarks were evenly spread across negative and positive dimensions.[10] The content of comments suggests that personal choice and empowerment, or its curtailment, are central to how OT is experienced. The attitude of staff and the nature of activities were also important factors. Examples are given below of negative comments, and these are followed by positive ones.

Negative

Activities were frequently cancelled and nothing put in their place. No attempt was made to suit patients' own interests, you were simply slotted in to whatever was happening.

They stick rigidly to what they have been taught and are not open to new ideas. Basket weaving is of no use for certain problems.

I hated having to do institutionalised things like basket weaving and also playing silly games like bingo. At the time, I was making a patchwork bedspread, but they wouldn't let me take that in to do. Everything was pitched at a very low level of intelligence. When I complained to my psychiatrist, he laughed and said 'you'll just have to put up with it.'

In general it was clear that staff knew very little about the crafts. There was little equipment – they spend most of the time chatting with each other. In one hospital I was only allowed to do 'female' type OT.

It kept me occupied but didn't sort out any of the real issues. There could have been more of a choice for people couldn't there?

Positive

Positive comments were often made about less traditionally run OT departments, as illustrated in most of the comments below.

Individual help was very useful. Ready to listen and not dominated by psychiatry.

More helpful than any drug treatment. Training in life skills really essential and totally helpful. Creative therapy is character developing – deals with an individual's emotions.

Taught me to pick things up for myself in jumble sales. They really taught me to begin communicating even in a very small way by getting me to do things that I couldn't have done on my own.

I decided what I wanted to do and they left me to do my personal project with their help in peace.

One OT group – a women's group for talking about problems was very helpful and has now become a permanent evening group out of the hospital.

I needed stimulus to trigger me out of the very deep almost unshakeable depression. Even 15 minutes thinking about something else was a blessed relief. It also helped curb my manic habits by doing something else. It was quite good to get to know other people and find self-help groups and other networks of what was going on in the community.

Industrial therapy

IT is more orientated in its aims towards direct employment than OT. It is usually undertaken after, as well as before, discharge from hospital. Just over one-fifth (119 people) of the respondents had attended IT schemes. Attenders were usually those who had had a number of admissions to hospital. Nearly half of the IT attenders had had 3 or more hospital admissions and over half (54 per cent) had total in-patient 'careers' of more than one year. The age group most likely to have participated in IT were by no means at the end of their potential working lives (32 per cent of the IT participants were aged between 31 and 40). There was a sex-bias in the provision of IT: two-thirds of the group were men.

One possible explanation for this imbalance is that selection criteria are orientated to an outmoded conception that only men need retraining for 'real' jobs, and that women should be content with a more limited domestic role. It may also be the case that women are less likely to value this form of training, or are less likely to view it as a positive means of social support in the way that men do. Other results from the survey suggest that women are more likely than men to use informal support networks and therefore do not look towards IT to provide this. However, there was also some evidence to suggest that the women in the sample were more likely than men to find employment after admission to hospital. When asked where their main source of current income came from, 22 per cent of women compared to 11 per cent of men reported that it came from a job.

Given that the primary aim of IT is vocational in orientation, most schemes attended by the respondents were unsatisfactory. They did not make contact with other types of agencies concerned with employment, and neither did they imitate authentic work-place environments. Most IT (93 per cent) took place on psychiatric hospital or DGH sites.

Most people attending IT (61 per cent) found it 'helpful'. However, it seems that this was not related to preparing people for, or substituting for, ordinary employment. This is indicated by two sets of findings. First, only a minority of people (46 per cent) identified this as the main reason for attendance. This reflects a realistic pessimism on the part of users that IT schemes are not able to deliver what they claim. Second, as Figure 5.2 indicates, the most useful aspect of this type of provision for attenders is not directly related to formally stated objectives. Once more the most helpful aspects of IT are deemed to be having 'something to do', followed by 'the company of others', whilst 'learning new skills' and 'staff assistace' were ranked a poor third and fourth.

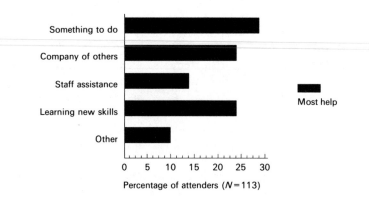

Figure 5.2 Perceived usefulness of industrial therapy

Eighty-four people made extra comments about IT. Of these qualitative responses, more were negative than positive.[11] Broadly the two main complaints about IT were:

Work tasks were boring

Many of the negative comments alluded to the tedious, repetitive or boring nature of the tasks they were set, as shown by these examples:

Packed crayons all day every day. Didn't need brain power because it was boring and tedious. No communication with fellow patients or staff.

I was hopeful that IT would lead to employment. However, carpentry, woodwork and in particular sanding wood was not my idea of being relevant to getting a job. I left before the end of the training.

The worst aspect was the mundane work – it's terribly mundane.

Hated counting nails and putting them into bags. Also didn't like putting the beans into bean bags.

Having to put little screws into little holes is head wrecking – it's equal to being locked up in a cell.

I have never known such boring work in my life.

The work is an insult to most patients' intelligence.

Exploitation and degradation

There were indications that rather than IT providing re-training and a fresh start for people who had suffered from the vagaries of a crisis and periods of hospitalisation, many experienced being further devalued. Apart from the tedium of the work tasks themselves, many people considered the system to be exploitative and degrading.

Pay was not very good – Monday to Friday for only £3 per week.

Not enough pay, no variety, patients are exploited.

Tedious slave labour. The pay system is a complete insult.

It seemed irrelevant to my condition and simply a way of getting little jobs done on the cheap. I was in the printing department and the staff there weren't really interested or were unskilled in talking to people.

Found the experience humiliating and worthless.

Positive comments seemed to be related to the absence of trivial tedious tasks and a more imaginative approach to IT.

Part of it was working on community projects which was particularly enjoyable.

This scheme trained us as responsible human beings being capable of doing the task.

I enjoyed most of my time in IT. Most of all I enjoyed my clerical post as I used to make contact with factories with regard to work for other patients.

Great encouragement was given by work-shop staff. I enjoyed the work itself and was treated with respect.

A number of responses indicated that there was some appreciation in 'getting paid', however small the amount, as opposed to receiving welfare benefits.

In addition to the subjective views of users, the outcome of OT and IT can be judged by the extent to which they created employment. As was discussed earlier, this apsect was an overall failure since the vast majority of people, who were employed before their mental health crisis, did not return to work. Those undergoing IT seemed no more likely to improve their job opportunities than those who had not attended. Though it is possible that this may in part be related to the 'chronicity' of some of this group (54 per cent had total in-patient careers of more than one year) this was certainly not the case for a substantial number of people attending IT schemes. The failure of IT to fulfil employment needs is indicated by a number of findings.

1. Only 12 people reported moving directly from the industrial training unit into paid employment.
2. Though a larger number (54) felt that it had improved their chances of finding a job in the long term, this still constitutes less than half of those who attended IT schemes.
3. At the time of the survey 67 per cent of the IT group were in receipt of some form of welfare benefit.[12] Only 7 per cent cited a job as providing their main means of livelihood.

4. During training the majority of IT attenders (57 per cent) got the impression that IT would not help people move on to paid employment.

Why are occupational and industrial therapists employed?

One of the points made at the beginning of this section was that, to a large extent, employment opportunities for ex-patients are rooted in general societal and macro-economic conditions. These arguably lie outside the direct scope of mental health workers and services. However, what is evident from the results of the survey is the limited and ineffectual role that mental health workers have had in stimulating work opportunities, even in a circumscribed way. Unlike many good practices in the area of learning difficulties in the UK and in mental health schemes abroad, OT and IT here remain firmly rooted in hospital settings. Only two conclusions can be drawn. Either these mental health workers should model their schemes on the good practices developed elsewhere, or the need for their own employment should be questioned.

The experience of users suggests little in the way of their service providers making contact with trade unions or employers or, even less ambitiously, ordinary employment training schemes in local communities. In this respect there seems to be a great deal to learn from abroad, where there are numerous examples of vocational and rehabilitation schemes which focus directly on mobilising employment opportunities. An important feature of the Italian experience was negotiation at local level with trade unions and employers. Workers' co-operatives formed a major element of mental health reforms in Rome and Turin.[13] In the United States, too, Warner[14] identifies a number of schemes which concern direct negotiations and the involvement of local business. For this to happen, it is necessary for staff to look beyond the confines of their existing stigmatised and segregated schemes.

Experiences of moving from the hospital to the community

The ability of institutions to deskill, disempower and create dependency has been central to arguments for hospital run-down and closure. Thus adequate preparation for discharge from hospital and resuming life outside should be a routine and prioritised part of in-patient services. It is likely that even short periods of hospitalisation can lead to the worst aspects of institutionally created disability. Even those who had been in hospital briefly reported feelings of powerlessness and a fear of trying to pick up the pieces outside. Moreover, a basic confidence in maintaining an existence outside, in relation to employment and accommodation, can be quickly eroded.

Undoubtedly those who have been in hospital for longer periods will have suffered the effects of institutionalisation and disconnectedness from their previous lives much more than those who have been there for shorter periods. With this in mind, those who had reported a one year or more in-patient stay on their last admission to hospital were used to gain a picture of preparations to leave hospital, as a way of gauging the challenge of discharge for both staff and patients. This group constituted 40 in all, who tended to be older than the rest of the people in the survey.[15]

Rehabilitation

As can be seen from Figure 5.3, people who were due to be discharged were generally given little prior notice. The reasons why patients were not told of such a major personal development beforehand is not clear. It may have been that discharge arrangements had been made some time in advance but that the staff withheld this information, perhaps on the basis that it would be distressing or would unnecessarily 'worry' patients. Alternatively, it may be that plans for discharge are not generally made on a systematic basis but on the *ad hoc* whim of the consultant psychiatrist and other staff. Whatever the reason, the length of notice seems inadequate to prepare patients for such a major change in relation to practical matters, such as arranging accommodation and informing relatives. Moreover, it leaves little time for the psychological adjustment that many will need.

Given these findings, it is surprising that more patients were not worried about their move back to the community. Seventeen people (42.5 per cent) were worried about living outside the hospital, compared to 23 (57.5 per cent) who said they were not. The types of worry expressed by patients were rarely about their condition; only one or two people cited coping with their mental health problem or deteriorating as the things they were most anxious about. Mostly people were concerned about how they

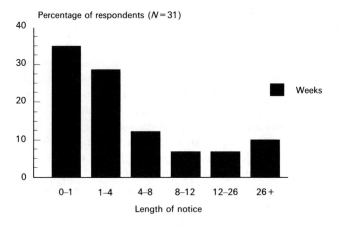

Figure 5.3 Notice of discharge for patients in hospital for more than one year

would 'cope', particularly financially, and about the short period of time they were given to prepare themselves for discharge.

I was worried about my ability to cope generally with my changed circumstances. The financial side was particularly worrying and whether I would miss the security of the ward.

Being prematurely forced out of hospital to detriment and trauma in integrating in an unknown community.

I worried about Giros not coming through, losing keys, living alone with no back-up support and generally not being able to manage.

Facing the public with the stigma of what was wrong with me.

Worried about leaving friends behind at the hospital. Had to get used to making new friends and I was worried about money.

A number of comments made by women suggested some concern about the domestic role they were under pressure to resume once back at home, as illustrated by this respondent: 'I was worried about being a housewife and mother again – how would I cope with a child who I hadn't been with since I got depressed.' It seems that, despite the often short period of adjustment allowed and anxieties about coping, overall people were positive about their return to the community. Certainly, this was indicated by the comments made by people about leaving hospital which are discussed below.

Even though periods of notice regarding discharge were often short, most patients (28) reported that hospital staff discussed their move back to the community with them. All but three people found such discussion to be helpful. However, there was apparently less recognition on the part of staff of the importance of the mutual support that people moving back into the community can derive from one another. Only 15 of the 40 patients reported being encouraged to discuss their discharge with others in the same position in hospital, or with those who had already moved out of the hospital.

Twenty-eight patients attended a formal rehabilitation programme to help them prepare for life outside. As far as the people attending these schemes were concerned, there appeared to them to be little recognition of the differing needs of individual patients. Only eight people reported having a programme of rehabilitation which was individually devised with them in mind. The rest reported attending programmes that were the same for everybody. Overall, rehabilitation was found to be helpful in preparing people for life outside hospital. Only one person said that he had found it 'unhelpful'. This points to the value that many people preparing to leave hospital derive from practical help with everyday tasks, an aspect which contrasts with the more professionalised, 'therapeutic' type activities favoured by most mental health workers.

Arrangements for accommodation

Not surprisingly, given the source of the sample, the largest number of people were discharged to hostel-type accommodation run by the voluntary sector (see Table 5.3). In the main it was social workers who made accommodation arrangements (for 19 people). Psychiatrists and voluntary sector workers were reported to have made such arrangements in six instances, reflecting the under-acknowledged role played by non-state services in de-institutionalisation. Generally, people felt fully involved in the decision to move into their accommodation; only five people reported not being fully involved. Similarly most people (35) were happy about the accommodation they were moving to and the ability to manage once there (24).[16]

Table 5.3 Type of accommodation people moved into

Type of accommodation	%
Flat or house alone	2.5
Flat or house with family	7.5
Flat or house with friends	10.0
Board and lodging house	10.0
Hostel run by voluntary organisation	30.0
Other	40.0

N = 40

Back in the community

In discussions about the pros and cons of the plans to close hospitals, very little attention is given to the views of users. Of the group of 40, with the exception of one lone voice ('I am very scared without the hospital – I want to go back there'), comments made about moving out of the hospital to the community were overwhelmingly seen in a positive light.

I had more fear of being in the hospital than being in the community.

Help has come from the community in the hostel not from the hospital.

Found life more active in the community than hospital.

I feel much more comfortable at the hostel; much better than when I was in hospital.

I was delighted to leave the institutional life of a hospital to resume my friendships and activities.

I am glad I came out. I have got on well.

The overwhelming support for de-institutionalisation policies on the part of those who, it is often claimed, have most to lose adds an important dimension to the debate on hospital closure. If, as it seems, people judge mental hospitals to do more harm than good, then there seems to be little support for the argument that patients would be worse off without them. This is not to say that people did not experience problems in moving out of hospital; they did. Nonetheless support for hospital closure was overwhelming *despite* the difficulties that people experienced themselves, or their awareness of the problems that fellow-patients experienced on discharge. Comments on people's move from hospital to the community revealed some of the problems that are experienced in making such a transition. One of the most frequent complaints was the lack of support people received on their initial move back into the community, as typified by these responses.

> I was discharged from hospital with nothing except an appointment to see a psychiatrist in a month's time. I feel I should have been visited by a community nurse — I had young children to look after. The social worker visited three times then told me that other people needed her more than I did.

> It was very hard to adjust. The day centre helped but after that there were no after care services or help — not even any information.

> I gained a council flat and more or less was told to get on with it. About the only person who helped me was my mother.

Often it seemed that, whilst users had felt adequately supported during their rehabilitation programme or attendance at day centres, there was no gradual initiation back into the community. Aftercare visits did not seem to be aimed at the systematic reduction of dependency, and often the type of help that was on offer was seen as inadequate. For example, comments were made that visits from professionals did not actually help them 'manage' with daily living or they were left to cope on their own. Certainly data presented in Figure 5.4 suggest that there is no automatic continuity of staff support when people move from a hospital to community setting. Whilst staff with a specific 'community' remit, such as Community Psychiatric Nurses (CPNs) or Community Social Workers (CSWs), generally started their contact with people during their rehabilitation in hospital and followed this through with contact after discharge, this was not the case for all professional groups. Perhaps most striking is the discontinuity of contact of the occupational therapists. Given that help with ordinary living skills is what many people seemed to want on their return home, and given that this forms the basic remit of OT, the lack of post-hospital input is particularly significant.

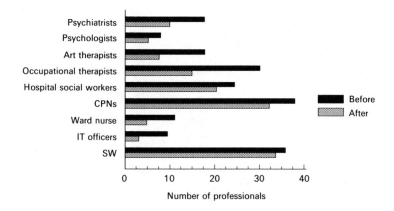

Figure 5.4 Continuity of staff contact after discharge

It is worth noting at this point that further comments were made spontaneously about community care by other users in the survey, in response to an open-ended question about services.[17] These comments also generally stressed a positive view of community care and hospital closure: 'The closure of hospitals is a good thing. The money from land should *all* go to community mental health services. We need properly funded services outside − such as emergency provision. It's our money from the asylums'. However, there was scepticism that decarceration policies would fundamentally change the nature of service provision. These doubts extended to expectations of alternatives in the community, the meeting of social and material needs, and confidence in a positive acceptance of ex-patients by the community.

Although in this area, our Victorian asylum has closed and been replaced by a purpose built psychiatric hospital, the actual treatment has not changed. Still not enough time given to counselling. Emphasis still on drugs and occupational therapy; still not enough help to enable people to cope on their own.

The government are not providing people with enough financially to cope outside of hospital. More should be done so that 'the community' will accept community care when people are moved out of hospital.

Moving people out of large to small institutions and then into the community doesn't solve their mental health problems. People get better but usually as a result of a good deal of security in their lives like getting a good job or getting married.

Not enough facilities in the community; not enough patients' councils.

Insufficient community care – especially crisis intervention and contact outside 'office hours'. More access is needed and general public need more education about mental health and community care.

Long waits for appointments with CPNs and social workers. Four months' wait for day hospital appointment. Not enough contact with patients immediately after discharge.

There are not enough alternatives to hospital. Good for people to leave hospital if there are adequate resources in the community. Needs to be much more available in the community. Hospitals are useful but only because that is the only place to go. What is really needed is people to look after you in a home environment – people who understand and will do the basics while people concentrate on getting better.

Mental health workers in the community

Although the data did not provide many specific details of the type of contact or help that each of the professional groups provided, the data does suggest, once again, that the way in which mental health professionals operate as a group tends to favour supporting patients from the territorial base of the hospital. Whilst there are widespread expectations that patients should learn to manage in the community, these do not extend to the professionals themselves: they have a tendency to remain wedded to the institution.

Notwithstanding the complaints regarding the lack of support and evidence of the lack of continuity of follow-through from hospital to community on the part of staff, examples of 'good' support both from professionals and informal sources were in evidence, as illustrated by these two comments:

> I have a community nurse which helped a great deal – particularly since the death of my mother. She has visited on a regular basis. Also the Samaritans have supported me at intervals throughout. My priest also calls to see me regularly.

> The hostel prepared me to live on my own in a flat, and the warden was and still is very helpful.

Some coercive aspects of hospital and professional management seemed to have been transferred into community settings.

> First I was refused OT facilities and was then sent to a day hospital against my will.

> The community people should be less heavy handed – they seem to be professional nosey people.

> When leaving hospital somewhere to receive advice rather than being told what to do would be helpful.

Users coming out of hospital were acutely aware of the intolerance towards them shown by neighbours and other people. For some, dealing with the hostile reaction of others was a major impediment to an ordinary existence.

> Once it was known that I had spent time in a 'nutters' hospital my neighbours gave me hell.

> I was unable to cut the grass in the garden of my new flat – it was overgrown and neighbours complained – this worried me.

> I was frightened that people noticing my odd behaviour would get me sectioned again.

> I was worried about coping with society and its expectations of me.

> I found a lack of understanding among the general public.

Years of institutional living had left some struggling to come to terms with sudden independence:

> The problem is people are disempowered in hospital to the extent they cannot cope when discharged.

> It was hard at first finding things to do and having to mix with strangers.

> I had a feeling of being lost in the community after the feeling of having been partially institutionalised.

> The social side was non-existent and therefore lonely.

> I was naive about the impact of 11 years in hospital. I could not resume an everyday life as if nothing had happened.

> It felt a bit strange coming out into the rat race. If it wasn't for my husband I don't know what would have happened. I had one visit from the head mental health social worker who gave me a card with his phone number on to contact if I wanted to. Otherwise I was left to my own devices and lucky for me. I had a very supportive husband plus two small children. I felt abandoned at the time and very isolated.

There was some evidence that lengthy hospitalisation resulted in an erosion of the resources that people previously had.

> I wanted the council house my mother and I had lived in before she died. I couldn't have it.

> I was persuaded by the hospital to give up my bedsit. They promised to find me new accommodation when I left hospital but they didn't.

As indicated by some of the comments made above, for many people relatives were often the only source of support once they had left the hospital. However, in terms of living arrangements at the time of the interviews, by far the biggest group lived alone (35 per cent), with 11 per cent living with parents. For others, a return to the 'family' home was deemed to be an unhelpful move, as illustrated by the next respondent:

Since residential accommodation is ostensibly aimed at increasing the independence of ex-patients, a number of questions were intended to elicit the level of autonomy and control residents had over their housing and living conditions. One of the most rudimentary ways in which people can have some power over their housing, in terms of the accountability of the landlord, is through the payment of rent. Most people (120), it was found, were directly responsible for the payment of rent. However, a substantial minority (65) had no direct control over rental payments. These were made directly to the landlord from the DHSS, local authority or, in a small number of cases, by relatives.

Other aspects of the degree of autonomy experienced by residents are indicated by the type and organisation of living arrangements within the homes themselves. This is particularly important in the light of the finding that this type of accommodation can be viewed as providing permanent or semi-permanent homes. Approximately one-half of those who had lived in residential accommodation had spent more than one year in this form of housing. Most of the residents participated in the preparation of meals (139, or 74 per cent). There was, however, far less control over other aspects of the running of the facilities. With regard to the choice of furniture and decor, the selection of new staff and residents, only a minority of the sample reported residents being involved in such decisions. Only 10 per cent (19 people) reported residents participating in the selection of staff employed in the home, although a slightly higher number were involved in decisions about new residents (28 per cent, or 53 people).

For 36 per cent of the residential group (67 people), a contract with staff was a precondition of staying in the residential facility. For most of these, compliance with treatment was part of the contract. A requirement to take oral medication was the most frequently specified treatment (for 82 per cent of the 67 people on a contract). Despite this being an obligatory part of staying in residential facilities, 67 per cent (45 people) thought that the overall terms of the contract were fair.

As can be seen from Table 5.4, overall satisfaction rates with accommodation appeared to be high, with nearly three-quarters rating themselves as satisfied with accommodation. Satisfaction and dissatisfaction tended to centre around two aspects: these were the physical features of the living space and the type of regime adopted in running the homes.

Table 5.4   Satisfaction with residential accommodation

Degree of satisfaction	%
Very satisfied	33.0
Satisfied	38.0
Neutral	10.5
Dissatisfied	11.0
Very dissatisfied	7.5

With regard to the first of these, adequate space, privacy, pleasant decor and convenient location, were, not surprisingly, the main aspects which appeared of importance to people. The following comments typified positive and negative evaluations.

> Better than any other accommodation I've had. Like a palace after lodgings.

> I had room to move around and I was not confined to a small space.

> Good cooking facilities, very clean place and close to town.

> Very comfortable clean new hostel, well run.

> There is adequate room in your bedroom to put things in. Facilities are very good.

> The rooms were small and tatty and there was only one room to socialise in.

> Shaving and cooking facilities were inadequate. I was dissatisfied with living in one room.

> I was in a women's refuge and found it difficult to cope with multiple occupation – especially all the children.

Comments about excessively rigidly run homes predominated over physical structure in the negative evaluations, suggesting that this was more important to users than the physical features of the residence.

Accommodation was all right but the way they were run was strict and certain rules were unnecessary. It depended very much on the individual who was running the place at the time.

I had to be out of the hostel between 9.30am and 4.30pm. If you didn't go by the book you were kicked out.

There are too many bosses here in the hostel. Sometimes by trying to help they actually make things worse.

I became ill and forgot my key, the worker on duty would not let me in. I went to the police and they got me in. The worker locked himself in his flat. I became angry because of his bad attitude which resulted badly for me.

No freedom of choice, no daily baths – limited bath water too regimented – rotas for baths and we were not allowed in the kitchen.

Equally, flexible, informal and homely-run houses were the basis of high satisfaction ratings amongst users.

As near to home life as possible.

It was well run by a caring and loving owner. It was homely, warm, and comfortable.

I was very satisfied because it's not so strict as hospital, the food is better and its a nicer place. It feels like my home and I get on well with the people I live with. Its nice being near to shops and having neighbours.

You have your own room and key – can have visitors to stay for overnight. Enjoy the company of staff and other residents.

Supportive staff – 24 hours on call, help and good counselling and advice about welfare benefits. Non-prejudiced staff.

Like it because all I have to do is keep my room tidy and wash my own clothes; there are no other rules.

Satisfaction rates also appeared to vary according to the agency that had overall responsibility for the residential accommodation. Not withstanding the smaller number of people who had experience of this type of accommodation, privately-run facilities were least favoured. Only 7.6 per cent (4 out of 52) of those in social services accommodation reported being 'dissatisfied' and 8.6 per cent (5 out 58) of the mental health voluntary organisation group. Both of these groups had positive satisfaction rates of over 80 per cent. In contrast to this, only 1 out of 12 people who had experienced privately-run accommodation reported being very satisfied with their living arrangements, whilst 7 out of 12 (58 per cent) reported being very dissatisfied. There were some indications that dissatisfaction with the private sector seemed to centre around the clash of providing care on a for-profit basis, as illustrated by these two comments:

The hostel was run as a private venture which ripped off the users.

Very like a pretty prison, discipline too zealous, run as a business not a care home.

There were also differences in autonomous living arrangements as compared to the rest of the residential group. In only one instance were residents reported to have been involved in the selection of new residents and the choice of furniture and decor. The preparation of meals involved residents in only 50 per cent of the homes.

It seems, therefore, that finer distinctions need to be made in terms of the evaluation of quality of living arrangements than a simple classification between 'private' versus 'public' provision. The high levels of satisfaction of those in mental health voluntary organisation residential facilities means they cannot be equated with privately-run ones. Equally it seems that not all voluntary run homes can be lumped together. Non-mental health voluntary organisations received less favourable ratings than those specifically set up with mental health needs in mind. This is illustrated by this comment about a church-run organisation. 'This was a hostel for unmarried mothers. I was required to have V.D. test. I objected to Church of England services — I was required to attend even though I am a Catholic. Had to be in by 5 pm and my boyfriend was not allowed on the premises.'

The pressure of poverty

Given the high rate of unemployment of discharged patients, it is hardly surprising that our data reflects the experience of living on state benefits much of the time. This chapter will finish by summarising some of this experience.

Whilst some disquiet existed about the actual efficiency and helpfulness of local benefit offices, it was the struggle of living on the sums received that provided the most telling criticism of existing income maintenance policies. Less than 30 per cent (27.9 per cent) of those responding to questions about benefits (N = 413) complained of benefit offices being either inefficient or very inefficient. A greater complaint was to do with who is a source of help about benefits. Only 38.5 per cent of this group initially sought advice from benefit offices, with 24 per cent approaching social workers and 34.8 per cent approaching welfare rights workers in the voluntary sector.

Welfare benefit levels and scales are set nationally and there is little scope for local flexibility. Amongst the participants in the survey there was a clear understanding that their levels of benefits are set by government and a consequent sense of anger and abandonment pervaded their comments. Many people used the terms 'degrading' or 'humiliating'.

It is degrading and causes more distress to the patient which in turn retards the return to health.

It is hell. It is demeaning. It is worse than begging on the street. We should have human rights. We do not. I invite any government minister to change places with me – not just for a week or two – forever. I am condemned to live this way. Could they?.

Terrible – feel like a pauper and degraded when having to visit the DSS [Department of Social Security]. This does nothing for your self respect. Feel like a scrounger.

Felt very much like a second-class citizen living in poverty. Unable to join in activities (e.g. sports) because of fares and fees. Missing out on many social events because of lack of funds, therefore losing social contacts.

Respondents were asked how easy they found it to manage on their welfare benefits during the periods that these represented their sole source of income. The picture that emerged was that the majority (nearly 70 per cent of 397 people) found it difficult or very difficult. Many of the comments shed light on how people sustain themselves and their families on limited incomes.

It is rough. You have to get your clothes from Oxfam. You don't have enough money to go out.

I've scrounged off skips – although the police say it's against the law – it's all right when the police aren't about.

In an emergency you are unable to cope financially and you have to turn to family and friends to borrow, which can be difficult to pay back. To survive on benefits you have to be prepared to buy from jumble sales or second-hand clothes shops and to economise on food.

Most of the time I can eat. Occasionally I cannot afford food.

I dread the electricity bill. I am lucky in so much that I do not smoke or drink a lot but I often lack money to go out on the evenings. I cannot afford holidays or records or books and most of my clothes are second hand. There is no way I will be able to afford the poll tax.

I would have starved if it hadn't been for charity shops, my mother and sister.

I have had to steal food from allotments to eat. I used to dry out tea bags and use them again. I don't think people realise how difficult it is to be a single parent on supplementary benefit over a long period of time.

No latitude for little extras like knitting wool, the women's institute, a ticket for the theatre. All these extras are essential for someone recovering from mental illness. Replacement of furniture difficult. Cost of heating difficult.

Conclusion

It can be seen from the data presented in this chapter that the quality of community living for psychiatric patients is a function of a number of factors: support from primary care services as well as hospital-based staff; gaining and maintaining employment; the utility or otherwise of occupational and industrial therapy; a sense of choice and control over accommodation; and finally avoiding or surviving the common pressure of poverty. When our data is set alongside the epidemiological studies quoted, which link recovery rates with social opportunities to return to a socially valued role, it is clear that the success of community care policies in the future will hinge on *all* these factors. In other words, a social policy on community mental health cannot simply concern itself with the resourcing of professionally delivered services. The prospect of a user-friendly future for service users will be discussed again in Chapter 8.

Notes and References

1. *Promoting Better Health – The Government's Programme for Improving Primary Care*, White Paper (London: HMSO, 1989).
2. Grimwade, K., *Counselling Within Primary Care* (Lewisham and North Southwark: Community Health Council Report, 1989).
3. See for example, Marks, I. and Scott, R. (eds), *Mental Health Care Delivery* (Cambridge University Press, 1990).
4. Warner, R., *Recovery from Schizophrenia: The Political Economy of Psychiatry* (London: Routledge & Kegan Paul, 1985).
5. 58 per cent of the men (135) reported having a job at the time of their mental health crisis compared to 47 per cent of the women (113).
6. However, this does not exclude unemployment having been a contributory cause where other main causes were felt to be responsible.
7. Sinclair, L., 'A Study Employing the Practices of Employers towards People with a History of Mental Disorder', unpublished report for MIND's Legal Department, 1986.
8. Ciompi, L., 'Catamnestic Long-Term Study on the Course of Life and Aging of Schizophrenics, *Schizophrenic Bulletin*, 6 (1980), pp. 606–18.
9. Warner, *Recovery from Schizophrenia*, ch. 7.
10. 85 were positive, 86 were negative and the rest were a mixture of the two or neutral.
11. 41 were rated by the researchers as negative, 21 were positive with the remainder being neutral or a combination of positive and negative comments.
12. Excluding those who were eligible for a state pension.
13. Ramon, S., 'Italian Democratic Psychiatry Ten Years On', *Open MIND*, 33 (June/July 1988), pp. 8–10.
14. Warner, *Recovery from Schizophrenia*.
15. 55 per cent were aged over 50 years.
16. One cannot exclude the possibility that these high rates of satisfaction might in part be due to a high number being accommodated in voluntary sector hostels and therefore these might not be representative of discharged patients more generally.
17. 'Please tell us your overall view about the current mental health services.'

6
Getting the Treatment

In this chapter we look at people's experience of psychiatric treatment. Under British mental health law the term medical treatment includes 'nursing, and also includes care, habilitation and rehabilitation under medical supervision' (Section 145(1), Mental Health Act 1983). This legal definition of treatment reflects and underlines the pre-eminence of the medical model and the medical profession in mental health services. Here we limit the use of the term 'treatment' to describe people's experiences of interventions that are specifically directed toward the control of symptoms, such as drugs, ECT, and various 'talking treatments'. Our data suggest that these treatments are experienced by patients as a fixed part the daily routine of services, rather than regimes tailored to people's individual needs or preferences. Most patients appear to have received most of the available treatments (in particular, drugs) for most of the time. Thus, whether diagnosed as suffering from schizophrenia or from depression, a majority (56.4 per cent) reported receiving anti-psychotic medication, anti-depressants and minor tranquillisers concurrently. Of those who received anti-psychotic drugs, more than half (51.9 per cent) received them as depot injections and in tablet or tot form concurrently. A substantial majority of the sample (78.6 per cent) had received minor tranquillisers and (48.5 per cent) had been treated with ECT. Major tranquillisers (or neuroleptics) are often known as anti-psychotic drugs. These terms are therefore all used in our discussion.

Physical treatments

It is possible that more people benefited from treatment programmes tailored to their particular needs and preferences than is apparent from the People First sample, but we doubt this. Our data echoes a body of research that identifies 'polypharmacy' and 'irrational prescribing' as a matter of 'continuing concern'.[1]

The concern about such prescribing practices focuses on two principal areas, the adverse effects of drug cocktails on patients and the financial costs of irrational prescribing. Edwards and Kumar also draw attention to the potential risks to prescribers in their comment, 'the adverse effects of psychotropic drugs are becoming an increasingly important medico-legal issue'. The adverse effects of psychotropic drugs can be life-diminishing, and occasionally life threatening. Minor tranquillisers are now well known to cause addiction in many people who take them in therapeutic doses over a period of several months. According to Tyrer[2] 30 per cent of people who take these drugs over such a period will have a withdrawal syndrome, 'panic, insomnia, tremor, muscle tension, sweating and palpitations'. More serious symptoms, such as 'epileptic seizures, hallucinations, paranoid delusions and the first rank symptoms of schizophrenia', occur in something under 5 per cent of all withdrawal reactions.

Sixty-seven per cent of the People First sample reported being prescribed minor tranquillisers. A study of self-reported side effects[3] showed that 77 per cent of past users of minor tranquillisers and 58 per cent of current users of the drugs reported 'bad' effects. The most commonly reported of these bad effects were drowsiness, lack of energy and impairment of memory/concentration. These effects need to be borne in mind in the light of the fact that many of our sample were often receiving tranquillisers in combination with anti-depressants *and* anti-psychotic drugs, many of which also have pronounced sedating effects.

The adverse effects of anti-depressants may be very severe, particularly in the early stages of treatment. The most common side-effects associated with anti-depressants are tiredness, dry mouth, blurred vision, constipation, impotence in men and reduced libido in women, increased sweating, palpitations and weight gain. Anti-depressants also enhance the side effects of both minor tranquillisers and anti-psychotic drugs.[4] Sixty-nine per cent of the People First sample reported drug side-effects as being severe to very severe. Despite the frequency and severity of such side-effects more than half the sample, 57 per cent, described the drugs as helpful or very helpful. Twenty-eight per cent described their drugs as harmful or very harmful.

More than 80 per cent of our respondents had been treated with anti-psychotic drugs and of those more than half (51 per cent) reported receiving them in depot injections and in tablet form concurrently. This is a higher incidence than those reported in prescribing practice studies: in-patients 18 per cent and day patients 13 per cent (Michel and Kolakowska), 32 per cent in-patients and day patients (Edwards and Kumar), 30 per cent (Clark and Holden), 37 per cent of a teaching hospital depot clinic sample (Johnson and Wright). The consensus amongst such authors is that, in general, the prescription of oral anti-psychotic drugs concurrently with depot injections is undesirable as it undermines patient 'compliance' as a result of increased side-effects. Patients are also exposed to a higher risk of the long-term iatrogenic hazards of tardive dyskinesia and dopamine receptor super-sensitivity (the iatrogenic hazards of anti-psychotic medication are described and discussed in Warner).[5]

Of those who had received ECT 42.8 per cent reported it as either helpful or very helpful, compared with 37.2 per cent who described the treatment as unhelpful or very unhelpful. Marginally under 20 per cent recorded neutral responses to ECT. The proponents of ECT see its main use as a treatment of serious intractable depression that may endanger the health or the life of the sufferer. Quite often the treatment is justified as an effective means of preventing suicide. Interestingly a standard psychiatric text, in discussing the suicide rate amongst mental hospital patients, notes 'the suicide rate among mental hospital patients in the United Kingdom remained steady for many years around 50 per 100,000 – some four times the national average. The introduction of ECT produced no change.[6] ECT or 'electro-shock' generates more controversy and vociferously expressed opinion than any other form of psychiatric treatment. However, drug treatments are measurably more dangerous in terms of both long-term health hazards and fatalities.

All currently available psychotropic drugs are pharmacologically 'dirty' compounds and have a wide spectrum of unwanted effects. Tricyclic anti-depressants are implicated in at least 10 per cent of deaths through poisoning in Britain.[7] (Although safer anti-depressents (SSRIs-selective serotonin re-update inhibitors) have been introduced doctors continue to presribe the more toxic older drugs.) The risk of death as a result of ECT has been estimated at 4.5 deaths per 100 000 treatments,[8] or approximately six estimated fatal ECT treatments per annum compared to at least 300 known fatal poisonings with tricyclic anti-depressants in Britain. Lithium has a wide range of unwanted effects and hazards including thyroid damage, kidney damage and weight gain (approximately 20 per cent of all long-term patients gain 10 kg or more in weight). Anti-psychotic drugs have a wide range of side-effects and hazards that include the occasionally fatal Neuroleptic Malignant Syndrome[9] and tardive dyskinesia.[10]

Talking treatments

Psychotherapy and counselling are broad terms which encompass a wide range of activities. The only definition of psychotherapy or counselling that might find a broad consensus of acceptance is that it may be referred to as talking treatments. Within this broad definition, activities ranging from brief supportive discussions with someone with little or no specialist training to intensive work with a highly trained practitioner over periods of months or years may be included. Within the UK NHS psychotherapy sits uncomfortably in the shadows of the medical model with its emphasis on physical treatments, such as drugs and ECT. Psychiatrists are the most powerful professional group in NHS mental health services. Psychologists, nurses and social workers and occupational therapists may undertake specialist training in psychotherapy and act as therapists within the NHS, but they are usually under the clinical control of a psychiatrist who may or may not have a specialist qualification in psychotherapy. Within the health service there are Consultant Psychotherapist posts but, as far as the authors are aware, none of these is held by a non-medical professional.

There is a high level of consumer demand for talking treatments as alternatives to drug treatments. This demand is most evident from people who have been prescribed minor tranquillisers[11] and is most often voiced in terms of a wish for someone to talk to about problems as a means of achieving insight, understanding, control and personal validation. Much more powerfully expressed is the need for support, help and respect from mental health professionals and from their communities. Whether meeting these expressed desires for insight or understanding will actually meet people's expectations or enhance their autonomy remains largely untested. Szasz (1979)[12] argues that psychotherapy is a 'myth'. He denies the validity of the concept of mental illness and thus the validity of any treatment aimed at curing or ameliorating it. Szasz describes psychotherapy as a 'metaphor' rather than a 'treatment', which 'refers to what two or more people do with, for, and to each other, by means of verbal and non-verbal messages. It is in short, a relation comparable to friendship, marriage, religious observance, advertising, or teaching.' (Presumably prostitution might also be included with Szasz's comparisons.) Setting aside the issue as to the effectiveness or otherwise of psychotherapy, people's strongly expressed need to be treated as individuals and with respect is self-evidently necessary for a caring relationship. Psychological treatments are more readily perceived as being responsive to individual need than physical treatments, which are often collectively administered in wards or clinics at 'medication time'.

Respondents were asked about their experiences of psychotherapy or counselling, but no attempt was made to define the terms conceptually in the questionnaire. The questionnaire sought information as to the type of agency or setting in which the psychotherapy or counselling was received. Respondents were also asked to make qualitative assessments of the talking treatments they received. We now look in detail at what our respondents reported about their experiences of receiving physical and talking treatments in turn.

The general experience of psychiatric drugs

Only seven of the People First respondents reported that they had never been treated with psychiatric drugs. 98.6 per cent of our sample reported treatment with drugs, whilst 1.4 per cent reported that they had never received drugs. Table 6.1 shows that the peak age for starting treatment with psychiatric drugs in our sample was between 22 and 42 years of age.

Table 6.1   Age when first prescribed drugs

Age (years)	%
Under 18	0.8
18–21	13.6
22–31	27.7
32–41	35.8
42–51	11.6
52–61	7.8
Over 61	2.7

$N = 488$

Table 6.2   Period of continuous treatment with psychiatric drugs

Length of time	%
Less than one week	0.8
One to three weeks	0.8
Four to eight weeks	2.1
Two to three months	2.2
Three to six months	3.1
Six months to one year	6.0
One to three years	22.0
Four to six years	11.7
Seven to nine years	11.7
Ten years or more	39.6

N = 487

Table 6.2 shows that more than 85 per cent of the sample had experience of receiving continuous treatment with psychiatric drugs for more than one year. A substantial proportion (nearly 40 per cent) reported continuous treatment with drugs of ten years or more. The length of continuous treatment with drugs correlates closely with the length of time that our respondents had been receiving psychiatric treatment. We interpret this finding as indicating that, for most people, starting treatment with psychiatric drugs represents the first step of a career as a 'psychiatric patient' in which medication is a central component of

Table 6.3   Longest period since first experience of treatment with psychiatric drugs that people have been drug free

Length of time	%
Less than one week	26.4
One to four weeks	7.9
Four to eight weeks	3.5
Two to three months	6.2
Four to six months	6.2
Seven months to one year	8.4
One to three years	19.1
Three years or more	22.3

N = 404

the routine of daily life. Table 6.3 shows the longest period people have been drug free since starting psychiatric drug treatment. Those reporting shorter periods of continuous treatment with drugs tend to be younger people with briefer psychiatric careers. This general picture is borne out in the following chapter which explores the issues surrounding consent to treatment.

Table 6.4 shows that about two-thirds of respondents reported receiving three or more different drugs concurrently, whilst marginally under one-fifth reported receiving five or more. Just over one-third of people reported receiving no more than one or two drugs concurrently. These figures tend to confirm the published findings of widespread polypharmacy discussed above.

Table 6.4   Maximum number of drugs received at any one time

Number of drugs	%
One	9.3
Two	24.5
Three	28.1
Four	18.0
Five	9.3
Six	4.2
More than six	6.0

$N = 439$

The experience of major tranquillisers

The use of the term 'major tranquilliser' to describe anti-psychotic drugs seems particularly inappropriate in the light of their widely reported unwanted effects, such as pseudo Parkinsonism and akathisia. Although these unwanted effects are well described as clinical phenomena, there is a paucity of literature that takes the patients' experiences of these effects very seriously. Therefore the account of two psychiatrists who experimentally injected themselves with a very low dose of a widely prescribed anti-psychotic drug[13] makes interesting reading. The experiment involved injecting themselves with 5 mg of Haloperidol (one-tenth of the lowest dose recommended for patients by the British National Formulary). Both described a marked slowing of their thinking and movement, together with 'profound feelings of inner restlessness'. Each experienced a loss of will and a lack of physical and psychic energy, and neither felt able to read, use the telephone or perform simple household tasks on their own volition, but could perform these tasks if told to do so. Neither experienced sleepiness or sedation; on the contrary, both complained of 'severe anxiety'. It was necessary for both to leave work for 36 hours until they felt able to resume their normal duties. If such a low dose has such profound effects on two presumably healthy subjects, it is not difficult to imagine the effects of the much higher doses given, often in combination with other drugs, to patients. What also appears to emerge from these accounts is that the drugs also induced a state of docile withdrawal from their surroundings in both doctors. Thus the tolerance that is said to develop in patients to these adverse effects may, to some extent, be an artefact of this drug-induced docility and/or the insensitivity of prescribers to such effects. Of 445 respondents answering the question, 81 per cent reported having been treated with major tranquillisers.

Table 6.5 shows that a substantial majority of people, once prescribed major tranquillisers tend to remain on them, while other figures show that 53.3 per cent of those who have been treated with major tranquillisers have received them by depot injections. These are most commonly administered monthly. Depot injections are most commonly justified as a means of ensuring patient compliance with treatment regimes, but it should not be forgotten that depot injections are a less labour-intensive means of delivering treatment.

Table 6.5   Longest period of continuous treatment with major tranquillisers

Longest period of treatment	%
Less than one week	2.8
One to three weeks	5.0
Four to eight weeks	6.4
Two to three months	5.6
Four to six months	6.4
Seven months to one year	8.1
One to three years	15.1
Three years or more	50.6

Table 6.6 shows that more than half (53.9 per cent) of the sample reported continuous treatment with anti-psychotic medication by depot injections for periods exceeding 3 years, the highest proportion of whom reported receiving continuous treatment for periods of 5 years or more.

Table 6.6 Longest period continuously treated with depot injections

Length of time	%
Two weeks	8.3
Two to eight weeks	3.1
Two to three months	1.8
Three to six months	3.5
Six months to one year	6.1
One to three years	23.3
Three to five years	12.7
More than five years	41.2

It emerged from our survey that 52.6 per cent of a sample of 228 people received major tranquillisers in depot injection concurrently with similar drugs by mouth or injection, which appears to confirm the extent of polypharmacy referred to by Edwards and Kumar, Clark and Holden, and Johnson and Wright.[14] Johnson and Wright make this observation: 'To combine different neuroleptics is to risk a wider spectrum of side effects without any potential for improved therapeutic response.' It has been suggested[15] that combining similarly acting anti-psychotic drugs in the same treatment regime allows for 'fine tuning' of the dose to suit the particular needs of the patient at any given time. In the light of the studies cited above we are sceptical of this assertion because such 'fine tuning' inevitably involves adjusting the dose upwards. We also are aware that many anti-psychotic drugs are prescribed PRN, or 'as required', and that they can be administered as a means of managing difficult patients rather than their symptoms. The Mental Health Act Commission notes in its Third Biennial Report: 'There are still many loosely drafted "as required" prescriptions which over a period may result in the administration of excessive doses with consequent discomfort and danger to the patient.'[16] Our findings confirm the grounds for such concerns. Table 6.7 shows that combination prescribing is closer to being a norm than a rarity in the experience of our respondents.

Table 6.7   Frequency of people receiving depot injections concurrently with anti-psychotic drugs by mouth or injection

Frequency	%
Very rarely	12.7
Rarely	13.4
Sometimes	16.9
Often	20.4
Very often	36.6

$N = 142$

The experience of the side-effects of major tranquillisers

Anti-psychotic drugs have a wide range of side-effects that include feelings of inner agitation, physical restlessness, feelings of detachment, trembling limbs, blurred vision, lethargy, dry mouth, sweating, impaired sexual function and occasionally the enlargement of the breasts and lactation. All of these, except the last three, were widely reported by respondents to the People First survey. There is a strong possibility that side-effects involving sexual functioning and the breasts were under-reported due to the sensitivity of such information. In a review of the literature on male sexual dysfunction associated with anti-psychotic drugs, Mitchell and Popkin[17] suggest that these effects drugs may often go unnoticed because either patients fail to report them or physicians do not ask about such problems. They also note that 'The available data suggest that when information is sought, such problems are frequently found.'

Table 6.8   Frequency of experiencing side-effects of major tranquillisers

Frequency	%
Always	25.9
Often	16.3
Sometimes	31.1
Rarely	9.5
Never	17.2

$N = 367$

Table 6.9   Severity of side-effects

Degree of side-effects	%
Very mild	5.1
Mild	32.9
Severe	43.8
Very severe	17.9

$N = 313$

Tables 6.8 and 6.9 show that a minority of people report experiencing side-effects rarely or never, and that a majority report those effects as severe to very severe. In the following chapter dealing with consent to treatment, our data suggest that patients are often not informed about side-effects by the doctors and nurses who prescribe and/or administer the drugs. We found a very low level of satisfaction amongst people about the nature and amount of information given to them about drug treatments. This failure to warn people may explain comments such as the following from our respondents:

Was overdosed with clopixol for 5 years by a psychiatrist. I slept for 5 years and put on four and a half stones in weight.

I feel that I am taking too much but I don't know what they are doing to me.

I wish they would invent one which does not put weight on.

How helpful are major tranquillisers?

Anti-psychotic drugs can effectively control or diminish symptoms such as delusions, hallucinations, social withdrawal and ideas of persecution, but they do not work for everyone. For some people the drugs are helpful most of the time, for others they are helpful some of the time and for some they are helpful sometimes but, for a significant number of people, anti-psychotic drugs have no positive benefits at all. Leff and Wing studied the outcome of maintenance treatment with anti-psychotic drugs using a large sample of people diagnosed as schizophrenic.[18] They found that 7 per cent had no positive response to the drugs and that 24 per cent of patients regularly taking them relapsed within one year. American research[19] reported that 5 per cent of patients showed no positive response to anti-psychotics and that between 10 and 20 per cent relapsed within the first six months of treatment. A more recent British study[20] showed that 78 per cent of patients receiving a placebo (dummy drug) rather than active medication relapsed within two years, compared to 58 per cent of those receiving active medication: a differential of only 20 per cent in favour of the active drug. Whilst such findings do show that major tranquillisers can be effective in preventing relapse for people diagnosed as schizophrenic, they do not give grounds for complacency about either the manner or frequency with which these powerful and hazardous drugs are prescribed. Notwithstanding the evidence of poor prescribing discussed above, our data suggests a production line approach to prescribing, rather than carefully monitored individualised regimes.

Table 6.10   Looking back, how helpful have major tranquillisers been?

Degree of helpfulness	%
Very helpful	17.7
Helpful	39.1
Neither helpful nor harmful	15.5
Harmful	14.4
Very harmful	13.3

$N = 361$

Table 6.10 shows that more than half the sample (56.8 per cent) described major tranquillisers as helpful or very helpful, whilst more than a quarter described them as either harmful or very harmful. A minority of people (15.5 per cent) recorded neutral feelings. Amongst the positive remarks made by respondents were statements confirming their effectiveness in relieving disturbing experiences:

If I don't take my injection I go haywire. I don't notice this but other people do.

They eased strange thoughts and feelings.

I think they did help me to calm down.

If I come off them I go 'high' but they squash my creativity, I get very tired and have no energy for ordinary things.

Some people reported mixed experiences:

I find twice in my life being turned into an overweight zombie, harmful and objectionable. The medication did clear up my symptoms (delusions, voices, etc.) but I feel I need this short term, i.e. I feel psychiatrists have a tendency to keep me on major tranquillisers too long.

I have only suffered side effects when my GP refused to supply Kemedrin® as in his opinion I didn't need it. My psychiatrist put him *right*.

In the qualitative data there were more negative than positive spontaneous comments about major tranquillisers, despite the fact that in the statistical results twice as many people describe the drugs as helpful. Comments indicating that people felt they were punished with medication are grounds for concern. Terms such as 'the chemical cosh' or 'the liquid straitjacket', which are believed to have originated in prisons, graphically describe how some people experience anti-psychotic drugs and how they can be used.

They were used as a punishment and to control my emotions.

Major tranquillisers were used as a method of punishment for non-compliance or for requesting discharge. Every time I was given MTs I was also given 'withdrawal of all privileges' — i.e. was not allowed to write, 'phone or make or receive any contact with any outside source.

If you get rowdy or excited you are forcibly given an injection which they make as painful as they can, i.e. seized muscles for up to one week.

Other people expressed further concerns:

Lack of concern from medical staff about physical and mental state since regime of tranquillising began.

Feel that major tranquillisers are overprescribed.

I feel that people should not be forced to take them because of the side effects.

Dull the senses and hide the problem.

Being made into the mental patient stereotype I found unbearable. When I managed to dispose of the tablets while keeping up the shuffling facade *no one* knew and said how well I was doing on them.

It's a 'hit and miss' game.

Feel that there was not enough care given in the giving of major tranquillisers. Often seemed to make me feel worse. Some tablets given which I didn't know what they were, but made me feel very bad. Felt very much overdosed on occasions.

There is a vigorous movement in the community at large and in the mental health service users' movement towards self-help. There are now more than 500 self-help groups in Britain concerned with minor tranquilliser use. Organisations such as Tranx, Release and MIND have put the issues surrounding the over-prescription and misuse of benzodiazepine minor tranquillisers firmly into the centre stage of public debate. The issue of self-help groups for users of major tranquillisers has been raised by the mental health service users and by some of MIND's local groups. Some have argued for the establishment of self-help groups for people who wish to withdraw from major tranquillisers. Others have expressed a need for self help groups for people who wish to reduce or monitor the doses of their own medication. If such groups are to be established they may need to be substantially resourced. Many minor tranquilliser withdrawal self-help groups function well with minimal funds and resources. Some people withdrawing from major tranquillisers may need a highly supportive residential setting with a high level of staffing. There is a risk that symptoms controlled by medication may re-emerge, or of withdrawal effects which resemble those symptoms.

Such resources are unlikely to become available in the foreseeable future. Resources are controlled by professionals who are likely to be hostile to their patients changing or modifying their treatment on their own initiative. Less controversially, perhaps, self-help groups might provide a means to reduce social and emotional stress, thus ensuring that anti-psychotic drugs are used to their maximum efficiency and in the lowest doses possible. Self-help groups might also develop as a method of self-advocacy amongst those on the receiving end of psychiatric treatment. There are people who might prefer to hear their voices rather than to experience the unwanted effects of anti-psychotic drugs (see below in the qualitative data). In the present climate there is little or no opportunity for individual patients to play an active role in their own treatment, or to negotiate with those who prescribe and administer these powerful drugs. In answer to the question, 'Do people think that self-help groups for people on major tranquillisers would be useful?', out of a sample of 393, 86.3 per cent said yes. This shows that the idea of self-help is attractive to a substantial majority of those who took part in the survey.

I feel people should be offered alternative support to major tranquillisers. Many people prefer to hear voices and find support rather than put up with the effects of drugs.

Unless you've taken them you do not know what kind of damage they do to your feelings and thoughts, particularly in high doses.

We need something like a union. It is too easy to write off the individual if he complains about his injections.

The experience of anti-depressants

No fewer than 74.8 per cent of the People First sample reported treatment with anti-depressants, whilst 24.2 per cent reported that they had not received these drugs ($N = 440$). Of these, all were able to recall the names of some (if not all) of the drugs they had received. The most commonly reported were the so-called first-generation tricyclic anti-depressants, amitriptyline and imipramine, and most used trade names when they listed their drugs: for example, Triptizol®, Domical® or Lentizol® for amitriptyline, or Tofranil® for imipramine. Some respondents listed nine different product names for different and similar drugs. It was striking to note that drug brand names rather than generic names were used by all but a small minority of respondents to list the drugs they had been prescribed: a telling reflection of the effectiveness of the marketing of pharmaceuticals. Brand names have entered the vernacular of psychiatric care. The side effects of anti-psychotic drugs, for example, may be described in Britain as the 'Modecate'[R] or 'Largactil'[R] shuffle; in the United States the same phenomenon is described as the 'Prolixin'[R] shuffle.

Table 6.11 shows that more than half the respondents had experience of continuous treatment with anti-depressants exceeding one year. More than a quarter of the sample had received continuous treatment with the drugs for periods of three years or more. Of interest is the finding that only 14.5 per cent of respondents reported short periods of treatment (up to 8 weeks). The first four weeks of treatment with anti-depressants is a critical period for most patients. During this time the side-effects of the drugs are often severe whilst their anti-depressant effects may be minimal or non-existent. Thus many people may feel worse rather than better during this time, and be more likely to abandon the treatment.

Table 6.11   Longest period of continuous treatment with anti-depressant

Longest period of treatment	%
Less than one week	2.8
One to three weeks	5.4
Three to eight weeks	6.3
Two to three months	8.9
Three to six months	10.1
Seven months to one year	9.5
One to three years	30.7
More than three years	26.3

N = 313

According to Johnson,[21] less than half of all patients prescribed anti-depressants comply with the treatment (that is, more than half stop taking their anti-depressant tablets); of those, between 30 and 40 per cent who stop taking the drugs do so 'because of the expectation or presence of side effects'. Between 20 and 30 per cent of people suffering from depression derive no benefit from anti-depressants.[22] In the light of these findings it appears that the compliance rate amongst our sample appears to be relatively high. This could be an artefact of our sample (all of whom had received at least one period of in-patient treatment) whose mental health problems can be classified as being more severe than those normally treated by GPs.[23] As such they might have been more accurately diagnosed and more appropriately treated.[24] However, our qualitative data suggests other possible interpretations for the high compliance rates amongst our respondents.

If you don't take the pills you get into trouble.

I recognise that I required some form of treatment but I believe that medication is overprescribed in psychiatric hospitals.

I didn't know what they were for or why I was taking them – complained but told to continue.

Drugs are handed out like Smarties without enough information to the patient.

Would have liked to have been offered alternative treatments. However at the time, grateful for anything to relieve mental pain. Antidepressants were preferable to ECT.

More than half of the 322 people had received anti-depressants concurrently with anti-psychotics (52.1%). In discussing the prescription of anti-depressants in combination with anti-psychotics, Johnson and Wright make this observation: 'It is clear that at the present time the prescription of antidepressants [with anti-psychotics] must be regarded as a clinical trial. Since there are possible risks of a schizophrenic deterioration these patients must receive careful supervision.'[25] In the following chapter on consent we show that only a small minority of our sample recalls *ever* having been formally asked to consent to a treatment with anti-depressants. It would be interesting to know whether the high level of combination prescribing reported by our sample reflects a nationwide clinical trial or, as we strongly suspect, pragmatic and undisciplined prescribing.

The experience of the side-effects of anti-depressants

Respondents were asked if they experienced side-effects whilst taking anti-depressants and to rate the severity or otherwise of these effects. Table 6.12 shows that just under half (46.7 per cent) of respondents reported side-effects as severe to very severe. This high level of reported severe side-effects must to some extent reflect the high level of drug cocktail treatments. The nature of side-effects reported included blurred vision; unpleasant taste in the mouth, numbness in the face, fingers and toes; weight gain; nausea; feelings of depersonalisation; increased depression; feelings of excitement; tiredness; trembling; constipation; headache; dizziness; pains in the legs; difficulties with urination; impotence; dry mouth; dry eyes and throat. These effects are the most commonly reported unwanted effects associated with anti-depressants.[26]

Table 6.12   Severity of side-effects

Severity	%
Very mild	15.7
Mild	37.6
Severe	31.4
Very severe	15.3

N = 255

Respondents were invited to comment in their own words on the benefits they gained from anti-depressants. More positive comments were made than negative and a few people expressed mixed feelings.

What benefits, if any, did you receive from taking anti-depressants?

They suppressed some stress, enabled me to sleep more easily. Benefits only after two weeks of treatment.

Helped with sleeping.

Improved sleep pattern, greater feeling of relaxation.

Helped me to see things in perspective.

Helped me to get back to normal life and feelings.

Felt very much better. Altered mood completely. Brought back appetite.

Overcame mild depression.

More confident and happy within myself.

I think they have dragged me out of the pit I was in. Kept me sane. Now I care that I keep well.

I benefit from not getting depressed so often.

Mood lifted gradually. Felt calmer. Felt that by being prescribed them the doctor believed me — that I needed help.

They actually seemed to help — feel satisfied it was a good idea to take them and didn't have any problems coming off.

Amongst the more neutral comments were:

Difficult to say if anti-depressants helped during the very deep depression. There were no noticeable changes, possibly a slight lessening of anxiety and worrying thoughts.

Would have preferred more information about side effects.

I don't know — but I expect they did some good.

I was told I would only be on them for six months and I'm still on them three years later. Would have preferred not to have been given false hope in the beginning.

Would have preferred not to take any anti-depressants, but have to rely on the professional competence of the psychiatrist.

Most of the negative comments, apart from references to side effects, were concerned with what people saw as the ineffectiveness of the drugs:

Been on anti-depressants for six months now and I am not sure of their validity.

It puts me to sleep at 6pm. I should be forced to live after 6pm at night.

Did not really find anti-depressants all that helpful. Perhaps they would have been more useful if I had gone for treatment earlier.

Felt they did little good.

Though the side effects were mild, the anti-depressants had no positive effect because they did not alter the original circumstances which had led up to it, and the current frustration I was experiencing, caused by those original events. I stopped taking anti-depressants long before my GP and the psychiatrist were aware that I had, and they noticed no difference.

As an out-patient I was prescribed and given large quantities of anti-depressants which I had taken as an overdose. Anti-depressants are very dangerous in overdose.

Anti-depressants weren't the answer. I realised it was up to me.

Minor tranquillisers

Here we look at people's experience of taking minor tranquillisers, mainly of the benzodiazepine group, such as diazepam (Valium[R]), lorazepam (Ativan[R]) and chlordiazepoxide (Librium[R]), all prescribed as anxiolytics, and other similar products prescribed as hypnotics, such as triazolam (Halcion[R]), nitrazepam (Mogadon[R]) and fluazepam (Dalmane[R]). These are amongst the most widely consumed drugs in the West. According to Spiegel, in 1986 the combined market value of tranquillisers and hypnotics in the West was $2090 million.[27] The extent of the prescribing of these drugs has been widely discussed,[28] and their potential for causing psychological and physical dependence is now generally accepted. A MORI poll undertaken for the BBC in 1984 reported that 23 per cent of the adult population of Britain had taken a tranquilliser at least once in their lives. Of this 23 per cent, 35 per cent (or 3½ million people) had taken them for periods of four months or longer.[29] A cross-national study by Balter *et al.*[30] reports that 5.8 per cent of the population of Belgium, 5.0 per cent of the population of France, 3.1 per cent of the population of Britain and approximately 1.6 per cent of the populations of Germany, Italy, the Netherlands and the United States are long-term tranquilliser users (defined as those who take the drugs for 12 months or longer). In considering the widespread long-term use of these drugs, factors other than their potential for causing dependence need to be borne in mind. Most important is the fact that after a short period the drugs cease to be useful. In the case of products sold as hypnotics, they cease to be effective after between 3 and 12 days, and in the case of anxiolytic products there is a lack of evidence to prove their effectiveness after four months.[31]

The Committee on Safety of Medicines (CSM)[32] reports that dependence on benzodiazepines 'is becoming increasingly worrying'. The CSM report makes very specific recommendations concerning the use of these drugs. They should be used only for the 'short term relief (two to four weeks only) of anxiety'. Long-term, chronic use is 'not recommended': 'They should not be used for the treatment of chronic psychosis.' In the light of these recommendations the reported use of minor tranquillisers amongst our sample is worrying: out of 443 people, 78.6 per cent reported receiving minor tranquillisers. Eighty-one per cent of all those were able to remember and name the minor tranquillisers, and again it was striking that, when asked to record the names of the drugs, people overwhelmingly responded by recording brand rather than generic names. As the issues surrounding the prescribing and problems associated with benzodiazepine tranquillisers have been so extensively covered elsewhere we decided against discussing these issues at any length here. However, we note that much of the discussion of the problem prescribing of these drugs has tended to point to GPs as being mainly responsible. Our data, and that of the studies of psychiatric prescribing cited above, point to a situation in which minor tranquillisers are frequently prescribed concurrently with anti-psychotics and anti-depressants in drug cocktails by psychiatrists.

Few respondents in the survey made any spontaneous comments about their experience of minor tranquillisers. The comments were mainly expressions of concern about being dependent on these drugs:

I suspect my depression is due to long-term tranquillisers.

I wish I had been warned at the outset of how addictive diazepam is and offered some alternative to repeat prescriptions.

I am now on a very high dose of Ativan[®] which I am dependent on. I was never told about the side effects and I am very unhappy about it.

Prescriptions given whenever demanded. When my tablets were taken off the market nothing given to replace them. Withdrawal terrible, thus adding to problems.

Glad that GPs are prescribing less minor tranquillisers. Would be better if GPs continued to be better informed. Glad that there's been a lot of publicity about the dangers of tranquillisers.

I like them because I can get pissed for half the price on them.

I have taken them for years, they haven't done me any harm (I hope) and I just can't sleep without them.

The experience of ECT

ECT involves passing an electric current across the brain in order to induce a seizure that is believed to be effective in the relief of severe depression. ECT was first used in the 1940s. The treatment has been in use for approximately 50 years but very little is known about the nature of its action or effects on the brain. ECT has continued to be the most widely and hotly debated treatment in psychiatry. In common with most forms of treatment in psychiatry it has been widely over-used.[33] Mortality arising from ECT has been reported to be as high as 2.9 deaths per 10 000 patients or 4.5 deaths per 100 000 patients,[34] rates that are said to be comparable to mortality arising from the use of short-acting barbiturate anaesthetics. Thus if ECT is over-used, patients not needing the treatment are being exposed unnecessarily to the risks of general anasthesia. Until quite recently there was a dearth of well-designed research into its effectiveness, but lately studies have claimed it to be an effective and rapidly acting treatment for seriously depressed patients.[35] In the United Kingdom the number of ECT treatments given has fluctuated over the past 8 years:[36] below are figures showing the total number of treatments 1983–89:

Year:	1983	1984	1985	1986	1987/88	1988/89
Total:	128 526	125 357	137 940	129 757	117 305	109 797

One of the more perplexing features of ECT statistics is the wide variation between regions in the rates of ECT treatment. In 1988 the rate for the Oxford region was 125 ECT treatments per 100 000 population, whilst in Wessex the rate was three times this figure (approximately 400 treatments per 100 000 population). Available demographic data is not sufficiently sophisticated to explore social class or environmental factors which might affect these regional differences. Nor do we know whether or not there are regional variations in the method by which this data is collected and collated. However, even within districts there are often wide variations in the rates of ECT treatments given by different clinical teams. Thus it would appear that the most probable explanation for the differences rests with the preferences of individual consultant psychiatrists rather than differences between patients.

A high proportion of our respondents have received ECT treatment (48.5 per cent of a sample of 464). According to the Royal College of Psychiatrists,[37] ECT is indicated for a minority of severely depressed patients. Table 6.13 shows that 43 per cent reported ECT as helpful or very helpful, whilst 37.1 per cent reported it as unhelpful or very unhelpful, indicating a polarised patient perspective on ECT.

Table 6.13   Helpfulness of ECT

Helpfulness	%
Very helpful	18.6
Helpful	24.4
Neither helpful nor unhelpful	19.9
Unhelpful	14.2
Very unhelpful	22.9

$N = 231$

Amongst the respondents who recorded negative views of their experience of ECT, a high proportion strongly condemned the treatment:

I never want ECT again. I am afraid of it.

ECT was forced on me and I was totally against it and will never have it again.

I gave my consent to ECT which in retrospect I wish I had not done. I think I would have come out of the depression some other way.

I think ECT should be banned. People should make up their own minds about having treatment.

ECT is the most frightening experience. I have had over 50 and still am very afraid.

ECT is inhuman. Sought psychotherapy privately as the only option plus self-help counselling.

Don't agree with ECT for myself — feel I have suffered permanent damage from it.

After ECT I was with another patient in the recovery room and found it nerve racking.

Given ECT forcibly without anaesthetic and muscle relaxant.

Side-effects of ECT

Respondents were asked to record in their own words any side-effects they experienced with ECT. The responses tended to confirm what is reported in the literature. Memory loss, confusion and headache were frequently reported.

Loss of memory.

Yes — memory loss. Confusion.

Confusion. Headaches. Loss of memory.

Memory loss (long term and indiscriminate).

Loss of memory. Affected cognitive thinking.

Memory loss. Fear of anaesthesia. Nightmares and flashbacks.

Terrible loss of memory of considerable duration. I had to retrain my brain to remember things. Mainly the worrying aspect was long-term memory loss where I could not remember things which I knew that I knew.

Memory loss for a couple of days, but comes back in time.

Headache. Dry throat.

Memory lost, spatial disorientation, massive headache and jaw pains.

Only side effect was that final treatments pushed me into a hypermanic state. Memory loss and headaches at the time.

Loss of memory which *didn't* right itself, bad headaches and sickness directly afterwards.

Only immediately after, not knowing where I was. It possibly had something to do with facial hair developing. It started about then.

Once it made me very ill and I'm frightened of ever needing it again.

Headache, temporary amnesia, concussion.

Can't remember.

Benefits of ECT

People were asked to describe what benefits, if any, they felt they had received from the treatment. Their responses were generally consistent but a few indicated that they had derived no benefit. A number reported the benefits as temporary or short term.

It seemed to stop the pain. I was more relaxed.

Worked – very effective; returned to work within 3 months.

Immediate relief from my symptoms. It's like a sledgehammer to crack a nut.

Shifted depression at the time (temporarily).

Helped me to become well.

Depression lifted very quickly after six treatments.

Lifting mood. Physical benefit, e.g. eating and sleeping improved.

Cleared my mind, helped me to get things straight.

I had suicidal tendencies before treatment. It helped to lift me out of depression – I received two courses.

Apart from ECT, I have not found other treatments effective. They are concerned with control of the situation rather than cure. I have been refused ECT on 2 occasions.

None.

Enjoyed floating sensation but still depressed. Received ECT six times.

It is difficult to say. After ECT treatment I still had a long stay in hospital on drugs.

None.

None – except for approx 3–4 hours.

Can't think of any.

None whatever, it's a crude form of treatment and risky.

A temporary lift of depression (shortlived).

It helped me forget painful memories of the past which were depressing me.

NONE, except cup of tea and biscuit when you wake up.

The experience of talking treatments

These treatments fared better in the eyes of our respondents than drugs and ECT. Psychotherapy and counselling are perceived as desired alternatives or adjuncts to a medical regime which obscures or denies the individuality and the complexity of the 'schizophrenic', 'depressive' or 'neurotic' 'patient's' needs. The main stream psychiatric regime also often seems to deny the natural curiosity or concerns of the patient about the nature of the treatment and its effect. A psychiatrist who described his own experience of in-patient treatment for depression made this plea:

> It may be that the doctor can only offer symptomatic relief or none at all, but sympathetic enquiry itself can help the patient by legitimising his complaints. It is easy for the depressed patient to become preoccupied with problems such as thirst tremor and clumsiness, constipation or urinary retention, which may be bad enough to cloud the picture of an improving mental state. The staff should also bear in mind the effect that the treatment, as well as the illness, may have on the cognitive function, as this may be an added distress for the patient who cannot appreciate what is happening or the fact that the impairment is temporary.[38]

Whatever the underlying theories or beliefs of the particular talking treatment, the process involves the service provider engaging in a dialogue with the service receiver. In so doing it implicitly conveys a sense of the legitimacy and uniqueness of the individual. We do not know from our data how the talking treatments would have compared with physical treatments in the experience of our respondents had they been more available or less marginalised in psychiatry. A number of factors should be mentioned in this regard. Currently NHS psychotherapy is still under the organisational and clinical control of psychiatrists (only this professional group can use the title 'psychotherapist' in adult psychiatry). This continuing dominance by the medical profession raises questions as to whether talking treatments constitute genuine alternatives to the medical model. There is a widely held view in medicine that psychotherapy compares unfavourably to drugs in terms of its 'cost-effectiveness'. In particular there is a strong tendency to treat those diagnosed as schizophrenic exclusively with drugs, and only refer those diagnosed as neurotic to specialist colleagues. It is clear from our data and from the demands of organisations such as Survivors Speak Out that, regardless of the diagnostic category into which people are placed, many service users want access to talking treatments.

Another factor that must be mentioned is the divided opinions amongst mental health professionals about the effectiveness of psychotherapy. Some — for example Eysenck[39] — argue that up to two-thirds of emotional problems resolve themselves spontaneously without the sufferers receiving psychotherapy. Research into the course of minor psychiatric disorders has ranked material psychosocial factors as providing the most reliable predictive factor as to outcome, followed by the patient's clinical symptoms and the 'genetic risk' scores.[40] There is persuasive evidence that anti-depressant drugs can relieve the symptoms of depression in between 65 and 70 per cent of patients. Patients given placebos instead of active drugs show a rate of improvement of approximately 30 per cent.[41] Such evidence of the efficacy of the drug treatment of depression is by no means unequivocal. As Spiegal notes, 'Although the number of reports showing imipramine, amitriptyline and other preparations to be significantly superior to placebo is higher than that of studies finding no significant differences, placebo was found in 31 of 88 studies (35%) to have a more or less equivalent "therapeutic effect".'[42] Presumably, even amongst those who did show a significant improvement over the placebo-treated groups in the trials cited by Spiegel, up to 30 per cent may have improved as a result of the placebo effects of the active drugs. Thus comparisons between the efficacy of drug treatments and talking treatments may not be as straightforward as the more enthusiastic proponents of drug treatments might suggest or imply. The evidence, such as it is, would not seem to support the apparent enthusiasm for the prescription pad in mental health services described by our respondents.

Talking treatments and physical treatments are not mutually exclusive in principle or practice. The efficacy of drugs can be enhanced by combining them with psychotherapy or psychosocial support.[43] Some of our respondents recorded negative views about psychotherapy or counselling, but many more expressed regret that it was not available to them. However, some caveats need to be noted here. Even reviewers who consider psychotherapy to be an effective treatment concede that not everyone benefits from it, and that some people's conditions actually deteriorate (so-called 'deterioration effects').[44] Of particular concern is any sexual or emotional abuse of clients by psychotherapists.[45] Arising in part from this documented abuse, some therapists and ex-therapists now condemn the unequal power relationship between therapists and clients and advocate self-help as a more relevant and safer alternative.[46] Our data suggest that if the mental health services are to be responsive to the needs and preferences of the users of those services, there should a greater availability of talking treatments.

The experience of talking treatments

Sixty per cent of 457 respondents reported receiving psychotherapy or counselling, but it is important to remember that this
can only be interpreted as saying that the sample reported
receiving some form of talking treatment. This finding needs to be
seen in the context of information given Table 6.14, which sets
out the professional identities, the agencies and the length of time
involved in the talking treatments reported by our sample. Of 167
respondents, 32.9 per cent wanted (but were unable to get)
psychotherapy or counselling, so marginally under one-third of
the sample reported wanting a talking treatment but not being
able to obtain it. Our data does not provide us with the ability to
establish why this was so. The general comments people made
about their experiences and views about psychiatric treatment
point towards the dominance of physical treatments (see below).
Some people referred to geographical factors:

I would have liked psychotherapy but it was too far to travel.

I would have had to travel to Bristol on public transport for
psychotherapy and I get panic attacks on the bus.

The fares to get to the group were more than I could afford.

Others spoke directly about the lack of facilities for counselling or
psychotherapy:

It wasn't offered in earlier years.

Requested psychotherapy, request denied.

Facilities lacking – not available.

One person said, 'I haven't got the courage to ask for it', whilst
another told us, 'I suffer from a psychosomatic disorder, i.e. lack of
faith – Jesus has the faith – the doctors don't.'

Who provides psychotherapy and counselling?

As we note above, the talking treatments may be provided by a
wide range of workers in a range of different settings. Table 6.14

indicates the providers of talking treatments received by our sample.

Table 6.14   Providers of talking treatment (%)

Provider	Yes	No	N
Psychotherapy/counselling from a private therapist	32.1	67.9	187
Psychotherapy/counselling from a voluntary sector practitioner	52.6	47.4	215
Psychologist/counseller working in GP surgery	9.3	90.7	172
NHS psychologist	53.1	46.9	211
Psychiatric nurse	51.8	48.2	199
Psychiatrist	52.2	47.8	203
Other medical practitioner	19.3	80.7	166
Occupational therapist	34.3	65.7	181

These figures indicate that people may have had psychotherapy and/counselling from more than one type of practitioner, but it is not possible to identify or further clarify the proportion who have received talking treatments from a variety of practitioners. However, given the proportion (60 per cent, or 274 respondents) who report having received these treatments it would appear that at least half have received them from more than one type of practitioner. The pattern that emerges from this table indicates that the most common providers of these services are voluntary sector counsellors, NHS psychologists, psychiatric nurses and psychiatrists.

Table 6.15 shows that less than half the sample reported receiving psychotherapy and/or counselling for more than 20 sessions, and almost a quarter received less than five sessions. However, it is difficult to interpret these findings given the looseness of the definitions of psychotherapy and counselling. It is not possible to make value judgements about the quality of talking treatments based on measures of quantity. Less than five sessions of psychoanalysis might be regarded as of marginal value by an analyst or analysand, whilst a similar number of sessions provided by a counsellor focusing on a specific problem might be regarded as being of considerable benefit by the practitioner or client. However, as shown in Table 6.16, there was a higher level of reported benefits and satisfaction with talking treatments than with drugs or ECT from our sample.

Table 6.15   Duration of talking treatment

Less than five sessions	22.3%
Six to twenty sessions	32.7%
Twenty or more sessions	45.0%

$N = 265$

Table 6.16   Satisfaction with talking treatments

Level of satisfaction	%
Very satisfied	41.3
Satisfied	32.8
Neither satisfied nor dissatisfied	10.9
Dissatisfied	6.9
Very dissatisfied	8.1

$N = 274$

Satisfaction with talking treatments

Table 6.17 compares the levels of positive comments (that is, 'helpful or very helpful' recorded in respect of anti-psychotic drugs, anti-depressants and ECT) with the positive comments in respect of talking treatments (that is, 'satisfied or very satisfied').

Table 6.17   Comparisons of reported levels of helpfulness or satisfaction

Type of treatment	%	N
Talking treatments (satisfied or very satisfied)	74.1	274
Anti-depressants (helpful or very helpful)	68.8	231
Anti-psychotics (major tranquillisers) (helpful or very helpful)	56.8	361
ECT (helpful or very helpful)	42.8	231

Negative aspects of talking treatments

As the following comments show, many people reported negative effects and benefits from talking treatments simultaneously. For example, many people found the treatment to be painful at the outset, but ultimately very helpful. Others saw no benefits at all arising from the treatment. Group psychotherapy or counselling was perceived by some people as being particularly unhelpful:

It was group psychotherapy, which when I became more severely ill didn't provide enough support.

Sometimes listening to disturbed patients got me down.

I did group psychotherapy in hospital first time I got ill. You were expected to be perfectly 'frank' and open with total strangers, albeit patients as well.

Frustrated because I feel they didn't get to the root of my performance.

I find group therapy depressing.

Negative effects from psychotherapy whilst in psychiatric clinic — conflict with other people during group therapy.

Group therapy in hospital was like being imprisoned in a nursery.

I was asked to attend a 'group therapy session' but was not given any info on what it was for, or what approach would be taken. The sessions upset me very much as I did not want to discuss my problems in the presence of others.

Other people complained that the treatment aroused feelings that were not adequately dealt with:

It was disturbing and unsettling. Like brain washing. Confusion.

Brought up a lot of issues we didn't have time to deal with. Finished when therapist changed jobs, finished very badly.

After each session (psychologist), following week became more depressed due to facing difficulties/problems.

It brought up a lot of problems that remained unresolved.

Others complained that the experience was painful:

It was like having a tooth pulled.

It made me feel worse. I don't know why, exactly.

I feel that psychiatrists probing and delving can cause a lot of distress.

I got upset.

Unpleasant feelings surfaced in therapy.

It has been painful and distressing.

I wandered around the streets crying after every session.

Some respondents were unconvinced about the value of psychotherapy:

Never got anywhere. Went over the same ground every visit.

No, just cynicism.

Was not helped. Still followed own way.

It took me 65 sessions to feel sure that I could not continue with the Kleinian analyst even though I felt unhappy about it from the first session. Like some previous therapists, he was convinced and wanted to convince me that I needed his help.

Didn't know what they were on about.

Delving into the past doesn't help me.

Yet others were not impressed by the practitioner:

Psychiatric nurse seemed to miss the point. Made me feel as if I had more problems than I said.

Analytical psychotherapy was done in such a way as to make me feel that my judgement was impaired in areas where it wasn't, i.e. insistence that transference had taken place.

Negative feelings due to lack of information, lack of focus on problems and feelings; analysing problems and feelings by psychiatrists in an inappropriate, destructive manner, i.e. 'being childish'; psychiatrist dictating what I should be feeling led to lack of confidence and further negative feelings.

The psychologist is very logical, which makes me feel good for an hour, then I feel confused.

It brought up things I was left to deal with when the counsellor realised he wasn't experienced enough to deal with them and couldn't offer any alternative.

Early in my depression, I started to have psychoanalysis from a psychiatrist in a NHS hospital which had a devastating effect because he dug around my past and I wasn't well enough to cope with it.

He told me to keep busy. I kept busy up till then but this has still happened.

The reported benefits of psychotherapy

The comments made by respondents about what for them were the positive aspects of the talking treatments sometimes contained more than one meaning. Thus a statement containing a positive message about the value of psychotherapy or counselling may contain an equally powerful and, to the individual, an equally important negative message about psychiatry:

Talking through the problem with student counsellor helped as it was better/easier to deal with problems after they had been shared. Acknowledgement of my feelings was very important. Benefitted from realisation that psychiatrist on a number of occasions, in my opinion, talking nonsense.

Understanding, validation and acceptance of experience from my perspective. Opportunity to talk over stresses in social and family life and traumatic experiences in psychiatric system. Complete confidentiality — seen as an individual, not a class of symptoms. Focus of discussion — my experiences from personal point of view rather than my behaviour from others' points of view. No value judgements made, unlike my experiences with nurses and psychiatrists.

There is more of a personal approach and you get to know your counsellor more so than you would your psychiatrist, and there is more time to discuss your problems.

Plenty of time. Different approach to that of psychiatrist. Give you advice in how to approach different situations.

I felt much more responsible for what happens, in non-medical settings. This enabled me to find ways of dealing with my difficulties.

I was able to understand my problems better, and given more information than was given by my psychiatrists concerning the reasons for my illness.

An explanation that I could understand of psychotic episodes. Continuity of care. A feeling that the healthy side of me was being encouraged and supported. Making it safe for me to be a bit mad sometimes without recourse to medication. Restored my faith in myself after negative psychiatric diagnosis.

Many of the comments above also contain other messages such as, for example, the need felt by people to be listened to as individuals:

He does not write anything down – while I'm talking he listens. Helped with confidence. Space to look at things logically.

Getting things off my chest. Being able to say what I like. Being listened to.

Space to talk and be listened to, a chance to build up my confidence in a non-threatening environment, a chance to discover myself and my potential. A place to be heard and understood, chance for personal growth, development and change. Chance for permanent change towards psychological health.

Somebody was prepared to sit down and listen to me and, although maybe not believe me, at least try to understand, and that was quite important.

Just that two hours of his time, and then followed hell.

Several themes emerged frequently time in people's comments, such as the need for comfort, reassurance and concern in difficult times:

> Realising that I was having an experience common to other people. Reassurance that I was not mad.

> Removal of feelings of isolation and uniqueness. Assistance with gaining self-confidence.

> Good to be able to alleviate problems by talking them through.

> I'm alive; I'm far happier than I've ever been; I feel more capable. I like myself; it was the first time I was able to accept that someone genuinely cared about me and valued me.

Many people referred to various personal life skills that they felt they had acquired from the experience of counselling or psychotherapy:

> Being given skills to analyse and understand feelings.

> Better able to communicate now. Better listening skills now. Positive feedback techniques. Reinforced view of life.

> I'm more on terms with myself now, I'm able to mix more freely. I'm no longer afraid to take responsibility, can show emotions without feeling guilty or embarrassed, and am finally able to renew family ties.

> Husband involved in part of therapy. We are talking more, trying to communicate better.

Finally, here is a comment with apparently contradictory messages: 'Someone was prepared to listen to me. I'm not sure if it was of benefit to me.' Perhaps this is a statement of the belief that, if something does not 'cure' the 'condition' it is of dubious merit, regardless of whether it gives relief from suffering or even brief periods of feeling a little better. The anti-drug lobbies criticise drugs because they only suppress symptoms at the cost of side-effects. The pro-drug lobbies criticise psychotherapy on almost identical grounds, except that the cost is measured in terms of the expense and cost-effectiveness of its labour-intensive and unpredictable results. But the message that emerges most powerfully is that people want to be heard and taken account of as valued individuals, rather than as the vessels of diseased or badly programmed brains.

General comments about psychiatric treatments

Here we look at people's responses to the question, 'Is there anything else you would like to tell us about your experience and views of the psychiatric treatments you have received? (Please use your own words.)'

Several themes emerged from these comments, but only a very small minority of people recorded comments that could be described as positive. Many people felt that their views and problems were not listened to. Even more felt that there was an over-reliance on drugs in psychiatry:

I was prescribed so many types of medication at one time they didn't work.

Talking would have been far more beneficial than any of the physical treatments.

Would like to have had more alternatives, e.g. talking therapies – psychotherapy.

Drugs given too often, treatment that doesn't take individuals into consideration. Not enough attention given to other ways of coping with mental illness, e.g. support groups – alternative medicines.

I recognise that I needed some treatment but believe that medication is overprescribed in psychiatric hospitals.

Not enough talking content with psychiatrists. All medication over-stated.

There should be more counselling with psychiatrists. A lot of my treatment seemed to be guesswork. Long periods without any kind of treatment in my stay in hospital, apart from being given tablets.

Treatment inconsistent, too many notes written which the patient is unable to see.

Many fears could have been allayed if things explained to me properly.

Original psychiatric treatment (in hospital) was humiliating, destructive and authoritarian. Later help to retrieve my shattered confidence was kind, well meant but ineffective.

In my experience the psychiatrists have studied the problem but failed to understand.

The psychiatric treatment I received could have been better if they had listened to the information I gave them.

I wish consultants would listen to the patients. Dr G. does. He's the first consultant I've had who listens to you.

I think that there is not enough research into these drugs as the side effects can be really cruel.

It may be that the drugs I take are a necessary evil in my life but I'm not sure if that's the case.

Treatment destructive and negative.

The consultant I was under longest was very unresponsive to my personal needs and did not give me enough of his time. In general treatment and staff were satisfactory. Some nurses and registrars were exceptionally good. Feel Haloperidol should be investigated.

I feel that doctors give tablets and injections because they think they are helping you.

I've always been quite satisfied with what I've received. I feel everyone has tried their best to help me.

Too much medicine and not enough talking and listening.

I think that on the whole the treatments have been successful. I am not as mad as I was. I am still scared of the bathroom. I need to work on my appearance.

Treatments should be explained clearly.

I feel the treatments are necessary and beneficial.

The comment of one particular respondent reminded us of the difficulties inherent in interpreting qualitative data. This person balanced the relative merits of psycho-*surgery* against psycho-*therapy* thus: 'One lady therapist seemed jealous of the fact that I had decided to have the stereotactic tractotomy rather than stick with her therapy. She said some very cruel and hurtful things.' Of course this intersting comment gives no insight as to what the psycho-surgeon might have said to the patient. Perhaps, more importantly, it raises important ethical issues that are not easily resolved in the climate of current scientific knowledge. In both psychotherapy and psycho-surgery there are more uncertainties than certainties about the measurable benefits and hazards of the treatments. Space does not permit us to review adequately the detailed scientific literature of either psychotherapy or psycho-surgery, even less attempt a comparative analysis of their relative merits; however, it is fair to note that in both treatments there remains more uncertainty than knowledge. This example of consumer choice illustrates an interesting potential clash of opinions between two treatment approaches that are often mutually antagonistic toward one another, organic psychiatry and psychology. Ultimately, it may be ideological rather than scientific factors which determine definitions of informed choice and which shape decisions made on questions of consent. We return to this theme in the next chapter when discussing those parts of the survey that focus on consent and compulsory treatment.

Notes and References

1. Sheppard, C., Collins, L., Florentino, D., Fracchia. J and Merliss, S., 'Polypharmacy in Psychiatric Treatment: 1. Incidence at a State Hospital', *Current Therapeutic Research*, 11 (1969), pp. 765–74; Skippard, C., Merliss, S. and Collins, L., 'Polypharmacy in Psychiatry; Patterns of Differential Treatment', *American Journal of Psychiatry*, 126 (1970), pp. 123–7; Herxheimer, A., 'Ignorance, Educating Doctors to Use Drugs Well', *British Journal of Clinical Pharmacology*, 3 (1976), pp. 111–12; Hemmenki, E., 'Polypharmacy among Psychiatric Patient', *Acta Psychiatrica Scandinavica*, 56

(1977), pp. 347–56; Marks, I., 'The Doctor, the Patient and Psychotropic Drugs', *Update* (May 1977), pp. 1195–200; Michel, K. and Kolakowska, T., 'A Survey of Psychotropic Drug Prescribing in Two Psychiatric Hospitals', *British Journal of Psychiatry*, 138 (1981), pp. 217–21; Edwards, S. and Kumar, V., 'A Survey of Prescribing of Psychotropic Drugs in a Birmingham Psychiatric Hospital', *British Journal of Psychiatry*, 145 (1984), pp.502–7; Clark A. F. and Holden, N. L., 'The Persistence of Prescribing Habits: A Survey and Follow-Up of Prescribing to Chronic Hospital In-Patients', *British Journal of Psychiatry*, 150 (1987), 88–91; Johnson, D. A. W. and Wright, N. F., 'Drug Prescribing for Schizophrenic Out-Patients on Depot Injections. Repeat Surveys over 18 years', *British Journal of Psychiatry*, 56 (1990), 827–34.

2. Tyrer, P., 'Benefits and Risks of Benzodiazepines. The Benzodiazepines in Current Clinical Practice', *The Royal Society of Medicine International Congress and Symposium Series*, 114 (1987), pp. 7–11.

3. Murray, J., 'in Gabe, J. and Williams, P. (eds), *Tranquillisers: Social, Psychological, and Clinical Perspectives* (London: Tavistock, 1986).

4. Lacey, R., *The Mind Complete Guide to Psychiatric Drugs* (London: Ebury Press, 1991).

5. Warner, R., 'Antipsychotic Drugs: Use, Abuse and Non-use', in *Recovery from Schizophrenia: The Political Economy of Psychiatry* (London: Routledge & Kegan Paul, 1985), pp. 239–67.

6. Mayer-Gross, W., Slater, E. and Roth, M., *Clinical Psychiatry* (London: Baillière, Tindall and Cassell, 1969), p. 805.

7. Heath, A., 'Toxicity of Antidepressants with Special Reference to Overdose and Suicide', in *Proceedings of a Symposium held in Stratford-upon-Avon* (Stratford: Franklin Scientific Publications, 1983), p. 21.

8. Royal College of Psychiatrists, *The Use of Electro-Convulsive Therapy* (London, 1977). See also Consensus Development Statement, *Electro-Convulsive Therapy* (Los Angeles: American Psychiatric Association, 1985).

9. Kellam, A. M. P., 'The Neuroleptic Syndrome, So-called: A Survey of the World Literature, *British Journal of Psychiatry*, 150 (1987), pp. 752–9; Abbott, R. J. and Loizou, L. A., 'Neuroleptic Malignant Syndrome', *British Journal of Psychiatry*, 148 (1986), pp. 47–51.

10. See, for example, *Tardive Dyskinesia: Report of the American Psychiatric Association Task Force on Late Neurological Effects of Antipsychotic Drugs*, Task Force Report Washington, DC: 1979).

11. The dangers and consequences of tranquilliser dependence have generated an extensive literature and the desirablity of talking treatment alternatives to tranquillisers is a constantly recurring theme, particularly in books written for and by lay persons. See, for example: Lacey, R. and Woodward, S., *That's Life Survey on Tranquillisers* (London: BBC Publications; MIND, Finding Our Own Solutions: Women's Experiences of Mental Health Care (London: MIND, 1986).

12. Szasz, T., *The Myth of Psychotherapy* (Oxford University Press, 1979), p. 1.

13. Belmaker, R. H. and Wald, D., 'Haloperidol in Normals', *British Journal of Psychiatry*, 131 (1977), p. 222.

14. See n. 1.

15. Ryall, D., 'Review. *The Complete Guide to Psychiatric Drugs: A Layman's Guide*. Lacey, R. Ebury Press. London', *NSF News*, 3 (1991), p. 5.

16. Mental Health Act Commission, *Third Biennial Report 1988–1989* (London: HMSO, 1989), p. 24(i).

17. Mitchell, J. E. and Popkin, M. K., 'Antipsychotic Drug Therapy and Sexual Dysfunction in Men', *American Journal of Psychiatry*, 139 (1982), pp. 633–7.

18. Leff, J. P. and Wing J. K., 'Trial of Maintenance Therapy in Schizophrenia', *British Medical Journal*, 5 (1971), pp. 559–606.

19. Cole, J. O., Goldberg, S. C. and Klerman, G. L., 'Phenothiazine Treatment in Acute Schizophrenia', *Archives of General Psychiatry*, 10 (1964), pp. 246–61.

20. Crow, T. J., Macmillan, J. S., Johnson, A. L. and Johnson, E. C., 'The Northwick Park Study of First Episodes of Schizophrenia; A Controlled Study of Neuroleptic Treatment', *British Journal of Psychiatry*, 148 (1986), pp. 120–7.

21. Johnson, D. A. W., 'Compliance-problems for doctors and patients', in *Antidepressant: Clinical and Research Update, 1986*, a symposium held at Malahide Castle, 6 September, under the auspices of St Patrick's Hospital, Dublin (sponsored by E. Merk Limited).

22. Ochsenfahrt, H., 'Second Generation Antidepressants: Therapeutic Effects and Side Effects Profile', in *Advances in Antidepressant Therapy*, International Medicine Supplement Number 10, sponsored by E.Merck Limited, 1984. Leonard, B. E., 'New Antidepressants and the Biology of Depression', *Stress Medicine*, 1 (1985), pp. 9–16. Levine, S., Deo, R. and Mahadevan, K., 'A Comparative Trial of a New Antidepressant, Fluoxetine', *British Journal of Psychiatry*, 150 (1987), pp. 653–5.

23. Sireling, L. I., Freeling, P., Paykel, E. S. and Rao, B. M., 'Depression in General Practice: Clinical Features and Comparison with Out-Patients', *British Journal of Psychiatry*, 147 (1985), pp. 119–26.

24. Brandon, S., 'Management of depression in general practice', *British Medical Journal*, 292 (1986), pp. 287–8.

25. Johnson and Wright, 'Drug Prescribing', p. 830.

26. Spiegel, R., *Psychopharmacy: An Introduction* (New York: Wiley, 1989) p. 14.

27. Spiegel, p. 235

28. Gabe, J. & Williams, P., *Tranquillisers*; Lacey, R. and Woodward, S., *That's Life Survey on Tranquillisers*.

29. Lacey, R. and Woodward, S., *That's Life Survey on Tranquillisers*, pp. 7–8.

30. Balter, M. B., Manheimer, D. I., Mellinger, G. D. and Uhlenhuth, E. H., 'A Cross National Comparison of Anti-anxiety/sedative Drug Use', *Current Medical Research Opinion*, Suppl. 4 (1984), pp. 5–20.

31. Committee on the Review of Medicines, 'Systematic Review of the Benzodiazepines', *British Medical Journal*, 280, 6218 (1980), pp. 910–12.

32. CSM, 'Benzodiazepines, Dependence and Withdrawal Symptoms', *Current Problems*, 21 (1988), pp. 220–8.

33. Consensus Development Conference Statement, *Electroconvulsive Therapy* (National Institute of Mental Health, 1985) p. 2.

34. Ibid, p. 6.

35. Johnstone, E. C., Deakin, J. F. W., Lawler, P., Frith, C. D., Stevens, M., McPherson, K. and Crow, T. J. (1980), 'The Northwick Park Electroconvulsive Therapy Trial', *The Lancet* (1980); Brandon, S., Cowley, P., Mcdonald, C., Neville, P., Palmer, R. and Wellstood-Easton, P., 'Electroconvulsive therapy: Results in Depressive Illness from the Leicestershire Trial', *British Medical Journal*, 288 (1984), pp. 22ff.

36. Department of Health, 'Electro-Convulsive Therapy Statistics. England. National and Regional Summaries for the Financial Year 1987/88' (London: Statistics and Management Information Division, 1989).

37. Royal College of Psychiatrists, *The Practical Administration of Electroconvulsive Therapy* (London: Gaskell 1989).

38. Anon, 'View from the bottom', *Psychiatric Bulletin*, 14 (1990), p. 452.

39. Eysenck, H. J., 'The Effects of Psychotherapy: An Evaluation', *Journal of Consulting Psychology*, 16 (1952), pp. 319–24.

40. Huxley, D. P., Goldberg, D. P., Maguire, G. P. and Kincey, G. P., 'The Prediction of the Course of Minor Psychiatric Disorders', *British Journal of Psychiatry*, 135 (1979), pp. 535–43.

41. Ochsenfahrt, 'Second Generation Antidepressants', p. 3.

42. Spiegel, *Psychophmacy*, p. 13.

43. Leff, J., Kuipers, L. and Berkowitz, R. A., 'Trial of Social Interventions in the Families of Schizophrenic Patients', *British Journal of Psychiatry*, 141 (1982), pp. 121–34. Falloon, I. F. H., Boyd, J. L., McGill, C. W., Razani, J., Moss, H. B., and Gilderman, A. M., 'Family Management in the Prevention Exacerbation of Schizophrenia: A Controlled Study', *New England Journal of Medicine*, 306 (1982), pp. 1437–40.

44. Lambert, M. J., Shapiro, D. A. and Bergin, A. E., 'The Effectiveness of Psychotherapy', in Garfield, S. L. and Bergin, A. E. (eds), *Handbook of Psychotherapy and Behaviour Change*, 3rd edn (Chichester: Wiley, 1986).

45. Brown, L. S., 'Harmful Effects of Post-Termination Sexual and Romantic Relationships between Therapists and their Former Clients', *Psychotherapy* (1988), pp. 249–55.

46. Masson, J. M., *Against Therapy, Warning: Psychotherapy can be Dangerous to your Mental Health* (London: Collins 1989); Smail, D., *Taking Care: An Alternative to Therapy* (London: Dent, 1988).

7
Consenting Adults?

Until 1983, British mental health legislation had provided doctors and other state professionals with the power to hospitalise and treat people deemed to be mentally ill without their consent. This power was inherited from Victorian legislation. The 1983 Mental Health Act supposedly set certain limits on this legacy, in the interests of the civil liberties of patients. As the twenty-first century draws near and the Dickensian asylums close down, our data allows us to review whether or not we indeed now live in a relatively enlightened period. Two questions in particular are of interest. First, are legal safeguards such as the Mental Health Act Commission and that part of the 1983 Mental Health Act concerning consent to treatment (Section 57) really effective? Second, if a patient is technically 'voluntary' or 'informal' (that is, not formally detained under the Act), does this guarantee them the right to informed consent?

Before presenting relevant data to answer these two questions, we will introduce a useful conceptual framework provided by Philip Bean[1]. This allows us to formulate a more accurate picture of the ethical and personal considerations that need to be taken into account when considering rights of consent in relation to people diagnosed as being mentally ill. Bean suggests that there are four aspects of psychiatric decision-making to consider in relation to the notion of informed consent. First, is the patient *aware* of him- or herself? Can he or she make judgements on his or her own behalf? Also, will those who *are* assumed to be aware of themselves (relatives and professionals) use that awareness to act morally? This aspect of decision-making is fraught with problems. How do we decide when someone is not aware? Even people who 'are not themselves' for reasons of mental distress may be able to make judgements on their own behalf about some things. But how do we disentangle or identify what these are? Also distress can be transient and this transience may be short lived or episodic. So it is not a clear-cut matter to ignore the rights that flow from self-awareness in these circumstances. Also, how do we know that others whose self-awareness is not doubted will act in a fair and reasonable way towards those deemed to be mentally ill? The answer to this, of course, is that it is by no means guaranteed in all circumstances.

The second aspect to consider is that of *information*. For a person to give informed consent to a procedure, they have to be told and understand what this procedure is and what is entailed in its implementation. Do professionals, then, supply comprehensible, comprehensive and up-to-date information to patients about the treatment they are receiving? Earlier in the book we demonstrated unequivocally that confidence is not inspired in this regard. More of this below.

The third consideration is that of *control and coercion*. As Bean notes, psychiatric procedures are all too often glibly described solely in terms of the positive or benign motives accompanying them (help, therapy, the amelioration of distressing symptoms, and so on). And yet, whether or not these positive intentions are achieved, formal detention under mental health law *always* entails an element of control of people, either in terms of deprivation of their liberty and/or the suppression or alteration of certain aspects of their conduct. Even those not formally detained are vulnerable to coercion in some ways. Formal patients may be forcibly injected or locked away in solitary confinement ('seclusion'); informal patients may be told that if they try to leave hospital they will be held under a formal section. If patients fail to co-operate with a staff-defined regime they may be denied privileges, such as wearing their own clothes. These are commonplace examples known (but not always admitted to) by patients and staff in psychiatric settings. Genuine consent to treatment would wholly or partially off-set these coercive processes. Coercion is a moral, not just a psychological, issue: that is, it is not only that it entails strong persuasion, but that it also takes advantage of a person's vulnerability or powerlessness. In the case of psychiatric patients, vulnerability is frequently present both because of their distressed state *and* because they enter a regime staffed by people who are used to exerting power over others. Like police stations, psychiatric hospitals or wards are places where authority permeates all procedures and communications.

The fourth aspect of decision making about 'mentally ill' people is that of consent relating to *a specific action or circumscribed set of actions*. Put differently, we cannot talk meaningfully about consent if it is a blanket notion. It cannot be consent to anything, but to something that is specifiable. If it were consent to anything then the pre-condition of information would not be present. The question, then, is whether or not the regime of mental hospitals ensures that consent to specifiable actions is always present. We would suggest that the accounts from our data throw considerable doubts on such an assumption. All too often being an in-patient is associated with arbitrary (and therefore unspecified) decisions being made about patients by staff. Doubts surrounding all four of Bean's aspects of treatment action will now be explored in the light of our data.

Compulsory detention and treatment

The picture which emerges from the respondents about information and consent is one which suggests a common disregard for patients' rights. It will be remembered that all patients in the survey had had at least one admission to hospital. Approximately 63 per cent of respondents considered that the reason for admission had not been adequately explained to them; 52 per cent received unwanted treatment (principally drugs, followed by ECT); 84 per cent were not offered a range of treatments to choose from; 68 per cent were not satisfied with the explanation they were given about their condition; 80 per cent considered they had not received enough information about their treatment generally, and more specifically 70 per cent thought that they had not received enough information on the side-effects of treatment.

Of those receiving major tranquillisers, 60 per cent were not informed of their purpose, and 70 per cent of this group were unhappy about the amount of information that they had received about their medication. No fewer than 74 per cent of major tranquilliser recipients had never given their consent to treatment, and 80 per cent of those who had taken major tranquillisers reported suffering side-effects, the majority of these (62 per cent) being rated as 'severe'. Around 86 per cent of this group also indicated that they would have liked to have been offered a major tranquilliser self-help group. Only 23 per cent of those who had stopped their drugs reported having any help from staff about the withdrawal.

The picture in relation to anti-depressants is similar: 70 per cent receiving them had not been asked for their consent, with 40 per cent having been 'persuaded' to take the tablets on a routine basis. With regard to ECT, only 14 per cent were given information about the purpose of the treatment, and only 9 per cent recall being told of any potential side-effects.

The qualitative data gives a flavour of what these figures mean to individual patients:

They listen but they don't explain anything to you.

Psychiatrists are not open enough. They do not explain enough about their diagnosis and how they view the interviewee's condition or discuss issues.

I think that psychiatry is a power struggle. The patients are treated like dirt and never told what is going on.

Once I drove my car to hospital for a supposed chat with a doctor and found myself locked on a closed ward and injected with Largactil.

I was threatened with ECT if I did not take Nardil.

Just told that I was to have anti-depressants and given them – no force but no choice given.

I was manipulated into saying 'yes' to an injection of Depixol. No information was given. The whole interview was handled disgracefully by the psychiatrist and my right to be treated as an intelligent human being was over-ruled. The hospital staff were reluctant to challenge the psychiatrist about anything. I asked the nurses questions about the treatment and they said I should have asked the psychiatrist even though I had asked him.

I have just been given treatment. I have neither been asked nor even persuaded. Some of the anti-depressants gave me burning in my throat, which is a very bad side-effect. Doctors don't tell you about this.

I was told that I would be sectioned if I didn't take the anti-depressants.

If oral medication was refused depot shots were used.

Once I signed up for a course of ECT but I was so drugged up I didn't really know that I was giving consent.

I remember the day that I hid in a cupboard to try and avoid being given ECT but they found me and made me have it.

No notice was taken of side-effects unless I screamed the place down and these complaints then led to being locked up in a side room.

Major tranquillisers (MTs) were used as a method of punishment for non-compliance or for requesting my discharge. Every time that I was given MTs my privileges were withdrawn – I was not allowed to write, phone or make any contact with people outside.

Are these impressions of life in the psychiatric system now in the past, in the wake of the 1983 Mental Health Act? Our study examined people's experiences of psychiatric services over time, with no restrictions on the age of the respondents. Thus, taking the sample in total, responses may reflect a regime in operation before the intended safeguards of the 1983 Act came into play. To check whether or not this was the case, we looked at a sub-grouping of 34 respondents who were under the age of 27 and who had been compulsorily detained. The picture painted by this group differs in no significant way from the sample population as a whole. Of course, most of those over 27 had experienced services both before and after 1983. We could find only two spontaneous endorsements, in reply to the open-ended questions from the total sample, that life had changed for the better over the years. Even in these cases, the respondents did not attribute this to legal changes. Thus, overall, the data does not suggest that the 1983 Mental Health Act has translated into improvements as far as those patients under its jurisdiction and supposed new protections are concerned.

Let us take, for instance, the supposed safeguard of the 1983 consent to treatment section. This requires that the reason for admission should be made explicit. Only two of the 34 younger people felt that the reason for being compulsorily detained had been explained adequately to them. Only two people were satisfied with the amount of information given to them by psychiatrists about their condition and the purpose of the treatment they were receiving. Only one thought that enough information was provided about side-effects. Only two people had ever been asked for consent to treatment with major tranquillisers. Ten of the 34 had received ECT, yet only four of these had been given any information about its purpose.

Does this imply that, with the exception of one or two patients, the rest were dealt with illegally? We do not know for certain, but it is quite possible that the 1983 Act itself offers enough 'loopholes' for professionals to exercise a wide legal discretion to favour their own power over patients. Whilst Section 57 prescribes the need for informed consent, other sections qualify this demand on professionals. Even when proper procedures are followed, subtle processes ensure that safeguards intended in the 'spirit' of the Act are not fulfilled.

Let us spell this out more. Under Section 58 of the Act a second opinion or independent doctor appointed by the Mental Health Act Commission is required to examine patients refusing ECT and to consult with a nurse and another treatment team member other than the treating psychiatrist before agreeing to the treatment. (The Mental Health Act Commission is a special authority set up by the act in 1984 in order to oversee its proper application to detained patients.) However, two processes militate against the patient's right to refuse treatment being upheld by a doctor giving a second opinion. First, he or she is likely to concur with professional colleagues about the 'need' for active treatment of patients. Second, the nurse and other team member are unlikely to dissent from a decision which itself has arisen in a team meeting. As with all small groups of people who have to work together regularly, conformity and consensus tend to emerge.

Section 58 also allows doctors to prescribe medication without the patient's consent for up to three months before he or she can then challenge the regime. (Even then the second-opinion doctor system then comes into play with the pitfalls just mentioned.) Another section of the Act provides the blanket let-out clause for professionals who wish to impose treatments against patients wishes. Section 62 allows treatments to be imposed if patients are deemed to be so dangerous to themselves or others that urgent action is required. Where the intervention is an injection of major tranquillisers, it is likely that it is used to control behaviour rather than to 'treat' the person's distress. Now, it could be argued legitimately that the temporary use of drugs to calm people down is in some ways less injurious than prescribing them on a long-term basis. Even if this is the case, the logical point still needs to be made that so-called 'urgent treatment' is typically about behavioural control. Thus Sections 58 and 62 together provide the legal conditions under which the spirit of Section 57 can be subverted.

Does informal admission mean voluntary admission?

Most British psychiatric patients are officially voluntary. Those who claim that too much emphasis is put on the coercive aspects of psychiatry often make reference to this picture from officially recorded statistics. Indeed, 80 per cent (412) of our sample had been admitted 'informally' at some time during their psychiatric careers. However, a substantial minority of this group (44 per cent) did not regard their status as being genuinely voluntary.

Comparing those who felt their voluntary status to be genuine with those who did not revealed the following points. First, there was a discrepancy about the number of people who felt pressurised into admission. The people who felt their voluntary status to be authentic reported being pressurised in only 21 per cent of instances, compared to the 'forced choice' group who felt pressurised in nearly 80 per cent of instances. In the latter case professionals were also more frequently cited as the pressurising agent.[2] The 'not genuinely informal' group was also more likely to receive unwanted treatment[3] and the reason for admission was less likely to be explained[4] to them than to those who regarded their status as 'really' voluntary.

It is also interesting to note that those who reported that their admission as informal patients was not a real one were more likely to be single and more likely to have been given a diagnosis of schizophrenia.[5] Bean's point about vulnerability is particularly relevant here. Single people are more likely to be alone and without support at the point of admission. Likewise, those with a diagnosis of schizophrenia are more likely to vulnerable because of their conduct being unintelligible, and therefore are hardly likely to attract the empathy or sympathy of others. Without a sympathetic social network to buffer them against the imposition of professional power, such individuals are clearly more likely to be vulnerable and therefore prey to coercion.

Informed consent and 'talking therapies'

It could be assumed that because talking therapies entail heeding the patient's experience rather than simply using it to elicit symptoms (as is the case in biological psychiatry) that this results in greater involvement in decision-making and divulgence of information. This assumption has recently been questioned by Masson,[6] particularly in relation to therapies derived from psychoanalysis. Our data cannot give a comprehensive picture of the issue of consent or explore many aspects of this contemporary debate about psychotherapy. However, our data does highlight a problem of lack of consent and information on the part of therapists. The extent of divulgence of information about the approach taken seems to predict the level of satisfaction people have with therapy. Whereas 26 per cent ($N = 121$) of those who had not been informed of the approach taken by their therapist expressed dissatisfaction with outcome, this dropped to 7 per cent of the group who had been provided at the outset with information. Of those indicating that they had been recipients of some form of 'talking therapy', 45 per cent reported not having been informed about the approach used by the professional.

Counselling and psychotherapy are not the exclusive domain of any one professional group, and they are delivered both within and outside the NHS. Private practitioners and those working for voluntary organisations appear to be slightly better at informing their clients of the type of therapy on offer. It seems 57 per cent of private therapists and 52 per cent of voluntary organisation practitioners appear to have informed their clients of the psychological approach they were adopting. Taken as a group those working in NHS settings (primary care counsellors, clinical psychologists, psychiatric nurses, psychiatrists and other medical practitioners) provided information to their clients less frequently (in only 37 per cent of instances).[7]

Here are some comments made about a lack of informed consent:

I was asked to attend group therapy but was not given any information on what it was for, or what approach would be taken. The sessions upset me very much as I did not want to discuss my problems in front of others.

Analytical therapy was done in such a way as to make me feel that my judgment was impaired in areas where it wasn't.

When I was seeking advice or opinion from my therapist I was not told about what the therapy was supposed to be about. There was no information. Also I found that the psychiatrist tried to dictate what I should be feeling. This led to a lack of confidence and further negative feelings.

The therapist created problems by implanting ideas into my head which were not there before. I did not understand what was supposed to be happening or what we were trying to achieve – it felt like a waste of time.

Psychologists were slightly less likely to inform patients of the approach they took than were psychiatrists offering psychotherapy. This may be because clinical psychologists are more likely to be eclectic in their approach and therefore find it more difficult to give a coherent account in each case with each patient.[8] By contrast, psychiatrists who train in the sub-specialty of psychotherapy are perhaps more likely to adopt a single (and usually psychodynamic) approach, leading to a greater standardisation of any introduction to treatment.

Discussion

Our findings on the picture of inadequate informed consent are consistent with research in the USA.[9] It should also be emphasised that research on informed consent in a variety of non-psychiatric settings also shows that the medical profession and those allied to it frequently do not clarify with patients what is happening to them. Indeed, in one study[10] it was found that psychiatric patients knew more about the side-effects of their treatment than medical patients did. However, the same study demonstrated that mental patients were less likely to be clear about why they are receiving medication. (Only one of 25 patients diagnosed as schizophrenic understood that they were being treated for 'schizophrenia', whereas six of the fifteen medical patients understood their diagnosis.) Other American studies of informed consent at admission show a similar picture to our own, with poor information and commonplace pressure.[11]

Whilst formal sections exist as a threat to non-compliant patients, it is difficult to deduce the actual number of people who feel that they are in genuinely voluntary relationships with mental health staff. Thomas Szasz has made the point that whilst there are legal statutes to allow forcible removal of mental patients from society without trial, it is not possible to conceive of a genuine voluntary patient. Our own data has simply confirmed what many mental health professionals will tell you about the 'hidden section'.

In order to have a choice, patients need both multiple options and adequate, understandable and accurate information about those options in terms of their advantages and disadvantages. Our data throughout this book show that the mental health system did not typically offer genuine options to the survey participants. Practitioners did not always offer understandable and comprehensive information about decisions affecting patients. In this light it seems that, all too frequently, genuine informed consent remains an empty promise for many patients.

The libertarian spirit guiding the formation of the 1983 Mental Health Act has not appeared to provide many improvements in patients' rights. What it has done is spawn a new layer of state-funded professionals (Mental Health Act Commissioners and their second opinion doctors) promising a limited watchdog role. Our data inspires little confidence that this role is always effective. This adds to a picture of failure elsewhere. For example, the scandals of the special hospital system have continued. The problems exposed by the inquiry into Rampton hospital in 1980 were simply replayed ten years later at Ashworth. In the first case, prior to the Commission, it was a television programme which uncovered the neglect and abuse. In the second case, after the MHAC had been in regular contact with the hospital, it needed the media once more to expose events. As a final example of ineffectiveness, whilst aware of the continued bad practice of polypharmacy, the Commission has not been able to halt its occurrence as our data make clear.

However, perhaps the greatest limitation of legal regulation is its inability to break the structural power imbalance which exists between professionals and patients. Whilst the original distress of patients may culminate, however it is treated, in prolonged disability, currently there are strong grounds to consider that some of the interventions of professionals (however well meaning) cause physical harm to patients, undermine their esteem and disable them from returning to a valued position in society. It is for this reason that users often talk of 'surviving' psychiatry, or of being 'survivors' rather than 'patients'. When distressed and out of control, patients offend everyday expectations of rationality and decorum: they can be frightening, perplexing, embarrassing or infuriating. This makes them vulnerable because professionals then assume a self-evident mandate to have power over this deviant conduct.

It is this starting position of vulnerability on one side, and the assumed right of power and control on the other, that risks the subversion of a principled respect for human dignity and civil rights. Once professional power comes to dominate the relationship, patients then have little opportunity to control their own lives. The mental health users' movement and their professional allies are the main source of hope to rectify the injustices arising from this power imbalance, rather than more mental health legalisation from the state. Advocacy and self-advocacy schemes in each locality may provide the type of real watchdog role which is currently missing. We will discuss this further in the next and final chapter.

Notes and References

1. Bean, P., *Mental Disorder and Legal Control* (Cambridge University Press, 1986).
2. In 65 per cent of instances, as compared to 45 per cent of the genuine voluntary status group.
3. 71 per cent received unwanted treatment compared to 47 per cent of the genuine voluntary status group.
4. For 71 per cent of the 'not really' voluntary group the reason for admission was not explained.
5. 31 per cent of the 'false choice' group were given a diagnosis of schizophrenia compared to 9 per cent of the genuine choice group. 72 per cent of the former group were single compared to 56 per cent of the latter group.
6. Masson, J., *Against Therapy* (London: HarperCollins, 1988).
7. This ranged from 15 per cent of primary care therapists to 48.5 per cent of psychiatrists informing their clients of the approach.
8. Pilgrim, D. and Treacher, A., *Clinical Psychology Observed* (London: Routledge & Kegan Paul, 1992).
9. Lidz, C., Meisel, A., Zerubavel, E., Carter, M., Sestak, R. and Roth, L., *Informed Consent: A Study of Decision Making in Psychiatry* (New York: Guildford Press, 1984).
10. Soskis, D. A., 'Schizophrenic and Medical Patients as Informed Drug Consumers', *Archives of General Psychiatry*, 35 (1978), pp. 645–7.
11. Klatte, E., Liscomb, W., Rozynko, V. and Pught, L., 'Changing the Legal Status of Mental Hospital Patients', *Hospital and Community Psychiatry*, 20 (1969), pp. 199–02.

8
A User-Friendly Future?

At the beginning of the book we discussed the difficulties which both professionals and researchers had found in taking the views of psychiatric patients seriously. We hope that we have broken free of these previous prejudices and set out the case for listening to the user's voice. In addition, in engaging with the data seriously, we have learned a number of lessons about the sociology of the psychiatric patient's view of mental health and a user-friendly social policy. These lessons will be discussed in this final chapter.

Conceptions of health and illness

This study set out to investigate users' views of their mental health problems, treatment and service delivery. How do the figures look in relation to other studies on the lay view of illness and disease? Some similarities will be considered next.

Lay views are more complex than the framework of illness

Lay understandings generally go beyond those of the medical profession by being more elaborate and taking a multiplicity of factors into consideration.[1] People in our study were likely to view their problems emerging as a result of a battle between 'endogenous' or individual predisposition (such as temperament, nature, inherited family features) and 'exogenous' factors related to a person's way of life (such as employment and domestic arrangements).

In principle, a rich eclectic medical psychiatric view might be compatible with this lay conception. Indeed, it has increasingly been argued that psychiatry does not confine itself narrowly to a medical model but adopts an eclectic view of mental disorder which takes into consideration social and psychological factors.[2] It is possible that this view is prevalent in psychiatric training and knowledge. However, if this is so, it did not translate into professional understanding as far as our respondents were concerned. The typical psychiatric formulation of personal problems tended to be construed in bio-medical terms (as indicated by the type of diagnosis and treatment given). In contrast, it was evident that contact with health services resulted, in the eyes of patients, from a complexity of cumulative personal and domestic events. Particular, precipitating or 'triggering' factors were often difficult to identify as a unitary cause of a 'breakdown'. People seem to experience mental distress as a continuum of everyday life, without an easily identifiable genesis.

A psychological emphasis

As in studies of physical health, patients emphasise the relevance of stress, coping, happiness and the ability to perform one's normal role. These personal or psychological factors were central to whether or not people saw themselves as experiencing a sense of personal well-being or developing mental distress.

Despite these apparent similarities with other sociological studies of the 'patient's view', there appear to be important differences in the conceptions of the causation of mental health problems when compared with lay notions of physical illness.

Less emphasis on illness

Fewer people were prepared to identify their problem as an 'illness', and generally to internalise a bio-medical view of their problem, than is the case in relation to physical illness. Problems were overwhelmingly seen in social, psychological and other terms. This suggests a widespread rejection of medical labels as an acceptable way of construing distress. The potential benefits of medicalisation, such as the removal of individual liability for the presentation of unacceptable behaviour, seem to have failed to convince users that problems formulated in bio-medical terms are helpful or comforting. Instead, they are generally viewed as unhelpful and stigmatising.

Although, as indicated above, people construe physical well-being in psychological terms, the degree to which users of mental health services view their predicament in wider existential terms is far greater. To explain the way in which people saw their future, comments about self-confidence, trust in others, financial and other social constraints or opportunities constituted the ingredients of their 'mental health problem'. In other words, it was not these factors which *led* to their problem; these *were* the problem. By existential terms here we mean that respondents saw their difficulties as meaningful in the context of their life experiences in regard to past disappointments, current dilemmas and future concerns.

Experts?

Chapters 3 and 4 described the relationships that people involved in the study had with psychiatrists, nurses and GPs. It is important to describe these relationships because they present a contemporary picture of the therapeutic alliance between 'professionals' and 'clients'. Additionally, general attitudes towards health and other services are formed in response to the experience people have as patients[3] and are thus important in understanding these users' wider views towards mental health services.

The attitudes of mental health users in this study differed in significant ways from previous research on lay views of health services. A number of studies have noted an admiring and respectful view of medicine, with a positive value placed on long training and highly scientific and technical work. This reproduction of medicine's preferred view of itself was not much in evidence from those participating in this study: in fact, quite the reverse. Being treated in a medicalised way, as if they had physical illnesses, formed the basis of negative evaluations and complaints on the part of most users in every aspect of their management. This ranged from a dislike of the aloof and cool attitude of psychiatrists during interviews whilst in-patients, to the rejection of physical treatments as a response to personal distress.

In summary, the professional discourse and the lay discourse about personal distress are incompatible (or 'incommensurable'). In this light it is not surprising that our respondents felt misunderstood and aggrieved so often.

Rejection of the hospital

The traditional territory in which mental health professionals operate was viewed with suspicion. Previous studies have shown that lay views tend to reflect the hierarchical structure of the NHS, with patients placing a high value on hospital-centred special-isms.[4] In these studies of physical illness a lower status is awarded by users to community and primary health care services.[5] The inverse was apparent in this study. GPs were appreciated precisely because of their distance from the hospital and orthodox psychiatry. The closer services were to people's normal living arrangements, the higher their apparent satisfaction. That users were overwhelmingly in support of hospital closure, despite the severe difficulties many of them experienced, was a further indication of their disaffection with hospital care. The medicalisa-tion of mental health problems, and the tying of resources for mental health to hospital services, might be professionally advantageous to psychiatrists, but not to their patients.

Social control

The lower satisfaction with nurses and doctors reported in comparison to studies of physical illness is undoubtedly linked to the coercive nature of the mental health services. Whereas these other studies have shown that professionals are not always perceived in a benign or helpful way, there does appear to be a unique aspect of mental health care services which accounts for their weak endorsement from their users. Much has been written about the social control aspects of health professionals. As long ago as the 1950s, Parsons' analysis of the doctor–patient relationship highlighted the social control function that doctors had in legitimating the entering and leaving of the sick role.[6] However, this type of control function is not only subtle and covert, often not being evident to the patient, but it is usually balanced by the perceived benefits that people obtain from health professionals in terms of care for, or cure of, physical ailments.[7] In this set-up the relationship is, with rare exceptions, conceived of as being voluntary by both parties.

By contrast, in psychiatry the control function is of a different order, and it seems there are fewer perceived benefits derived from medical interventions as we demonstrated in Chapter 6.

Training implications of the data

It was shown in Chapters 3 and 4 that a preferred model of practice would stress personal contact and understanding and eschew specialised treatments and techniques. Also, users endorsed the value of the informality and flexibility in the voluntary sector. This contrasts with their dislike of the constraints and formality experienced in the statutory sector. Moreover, the voluntary sector offers opportunities for attaining self-esteem and valued social roles through participation in the organisation and delivery of services.

Both these valued aspects run contrary to trends within professional training which focus on creating increasingly 'specialised' services and modes of intervention. High levels of 'skill' and 'expertise', whether in psychological therapies, medicine or nursing, run counter to the emphasis on *deskilling*, which is implied by what users identify as being beneficial: that is, if professionals were to approximate to the conception preferred by users, they would have to shed most or all of their pretensions towards specialised knowledge.

Social policy implications

We hope that the data presented throughout the book have drawn attention to two types of debate about mental health policy. The first debate is this: should the present medical model, with its coercive tradition, be transferred uncritically to the community; or should a new policy be endorsed which empowers users and emphasises voluntarism? The second debate is whether people with mental health problems are seen by policy-makers as being in need of a specialist services which separate them from others in society, or should they be helped to live ordinary lives in ordinary settings?

Broadly it is possible to deduce two possible futures for mental health policy from the data. The first (described below) highlights the outcome of the above debates favouring coercion and separation, whilst the second highlights the above debates being resolved to favour the interests of service users.

Outcome 1

Transporting the existing model lock stock and barrel into the community

One outcome for the future would have the following elements. It would simply extend into the community the existing model of psychiatric services which was set by Victorian psychiatry, and modified by a weak concession to voluntarism after the First World War. Despite a move away from psychiatry's traditional territory of the large and remote asylum, there would be a continued emphasis on physical treatments in hospital settings. The importance of coercion (rationalised as 'treatment') would also remain central, although this might take a different form (it might be disguised as 'community treatment orders', 'case registers' or 'guardianship'). Although professional interventions would continue to be mixed (eclectic), with counselling or psychotherapy perhaps taking a slightly higher profile than in the past, the central tenets of the contemporary service provision would not change fundamentally. In short, biological reasoning and physical coercion would continue to define the content of services, although its form would be modified as a result of working outside of institutional boundaries.

Of course, if certain lobbies win the day in current debates about hospital run-down and closure, then even the modest aspiration of operating outside the old Victorian asylums might not even be achieved by the end of this century. This 'nightmare scenario' would involve resources being split between the old 'asylums', new DGH acute psychiatric units and local authority community care initiatives. This is described as a 'nightmare' because no one party in this three-way split would be resourced to its own satisfaction. The problems of the 1980s, in which neither the old segregative nor the new de-institutionalisation policies fully operated, would continue. The difficulties would simply be frozen in time.

What seems to be an important question is not only whether or not hospitals will close but also the extent to which the coercive elements of these outmoded regimes are simply transferred into 'the community'. For example, in 1987 the Royal College of Psychiatrists, supported by the National Schizophrenia Fellowship (NSF), pressed to modify the 1983 Mental Health Act to include CTOs.[8] After much debate, this idea seems to have died a death for the time being. However, this example, and similar measures (such as an extended use of guardianship under the 1983 Mental Health Act), remain relevant because they could be disinterred and resurrected. Additionally, such proposals highlight the type of thinking and responses that certain interest groups are preoccupied with when 'care in the community' is being discussed. If, as the logic goes, emotional distress is a reflection of a bio-medical condition, then attempts will continue both inside and outside medicine to force medical 'treatments' on those who as a result of their 'illness' do not realise they are in need.

Another indicator that social control will continue to be a pressing issue for many is the campaign for 'registers' of patients after their discharge from hospital. Current trends indicate that British psychiatry could mimic the enthusiasm of its American colleagues for community surveillance and enforced treatment. Close surveillance and ensuring compliance with treatment seem to be emerging as integral parts of the 'case management' of people discharged from hospital. A model which combined these elements developed in the USA in the 1980s; psychiatric teams would track down patients in the community and force their ministrations upon them. Whilst a superficial reading of this trend is that it is in the patients' interest to have professional attention taken to them to enforce hospital admission, day centre attendance, drug treatment or all of these, it begs a fundamental question: if psychiatric attention is so necessary and so helpful, why does it have to be forced on people? Or, to put it differently, perhaps the evasion of professional attention reflects an understandable tendency for patients to vote with their feet. It may be the case that a small number of ex-patients may 'get lost', and would be grateful for being followed up in this way. However, the whole question of informed and genuine choice in professional work is highlighted by our data. Our respondents all too often felt coerced, and were not given options.

As far as the organisation of services is concerned, it is likely that this first type of outcome would rely heavily on utilising the DGH unit. Services would be focused on acute admissions, and physical treatments would be overseen by medicine. In other words, the old system of the large hospitals would, with a few minor modifications, simply be reproduced in a new setting. The length of stay would presumably be reduced because of the smaller number of beds allocated for the same number of patients, and many people would not have so far to travel, although even this should not be taken for granted. If services are built on one site, it is inevitable that this will provide an impediment of access to local people (compared to smaller, more scattered facilities)

Even the physical characteristics of the DGH unit cannot be assumed to be an improvement on the old 'bins'. DGH wards are normally smaller in their dimensions. They often have low ceilings and are in multi-storey buildings. The patients may be kept in their pyjamas to dissuade them from leaving the ward and offending physical patients in other parts of the building. In the old hospitals there were often spacious grounds, which is rarely the case in

DGHs. The medical priorities of treating physical illness also tend to set the parameters of what is appropriate for those with mental health problems. Many of these new units and wards have beds arranged as in other Nightingale wards, making any notion of privacy impossible. And since there is a preoccupation with beds there is little space for recreation or other uses. For example, plans indicate many will have new ECT 'suites', yet no designated appropriate space for counselling or psychotherapy. Thus, the restrictive environment of these modern hospital settings may actually be more oppressive than their predecessors. If the DGH also becomes the focus of day care facilities then the disadvantage is amplified.

If hospital-based services still inaccurately pass themselves off as a community care policy, then this will have two consequences. First, it will encourage policy-makers, and those responsible for policy implementation, to continue to frame mental health problems in terms of medical needs. This would be fine if medicine had a good track record in responding to distress in a satisfactory way. Throughout this book it has been clear that, as far as patients are concerned, this is not the case. In his review of British mental health policy since the Second World War, Goodwin[9] makes the point that government after government has mistakenly been committed to the notion that psychiatric treatment is sound and effective. The empirical evidence in our data and elsewhere underlines why Goodwin's conclusion is well founded. The recent legislation on community care continues to place all the power and resources in the hands of medically-centred health authorities. In other words, medically defined 'need' for treatment is prioritised and financed, and the social needs of patients are left in the hands of the under-funded local authorities.

Thus a further feature of the first likely outcome is a continuation of the current inordinate budgetary imbalance between the NHS and local authorities. In the run up to the 1990 NHS and Community Care Act, it was commented that the preceding White Paper (*Caring for People*) constituted a 'poisoned chalice' for local authorities. The latter had been given the overall responsibility to co-ordinate community care in practice but it had been given no guaranteed or 'ringfenced' funds to do the job. (The exception in this regard was the 'mental illness grant', which was a tiny resource capable of helping only about 12 patients in each District.) As Sayce, the Policy Director of MIND, noted,[10] in 1979 only 12 pence in every £1 was spent by the government on non-hospital services. By 1988 this had only risen to 15 pence despite escalating de-institutionalisation. Without a bridging arrangement, it can be seen what this leads to: community facilities are not prioritised and hospital facilities are depleted of finance in comparison to earlier times.

If this way of organising professional services continues, it will prevent the development of more flexible, locally accessible services for people in distress. Moreover, it will concentrate the minds of policy-makers and implementers on professionally-led medical services rather than on key social priorities, especially housing and income maintenance. In the light of these possibilities, what is the second scenario we might look forward to?

Outcome 2

A post-medical, user-led service

The second outcome, in a sense, would in many respects be the inverse of the first. It is not entirely impossible that alliances between users and enlightened professionals, policy-makers and other lay people might influence policy-making in a different and more progressive way.

In opposition to the first outcome, a different mental health policy would prioritise voluntary relationships, not coercion. It would produce a service which was shaped by user participation, and even user leadership. Most of the debates about the progressive reform of welfare provision (to make it more democratically accountable) centred until 1979 on the involvement of health and welfare workers. What the attack on the public sector by three successive Conservative administrations did, amongst other things, was highlight the democratic rights of *consumers* of services. Whatever rhetorical status the Tory slogan about 'putting the patient first' may have had, it has opened up new possibilities for disenfranchised groups such as psychiatric patients. The cross-party discourse is now about 'user-friendliness' and 'quality assurance'. The Labour Party, with its traditional tendency to defer to medical and other expert authority, is also actively re-thinking the role of the client in the welfare system. Thus new forms of democratic accountability are now firmly on the political agenda, and mental health clients stand to benefit from the debate.

It is possible that with the realignment of the status of users in policy debates, the philosophy relating to their treatment would also have to change. If users' views reported in this book were replicated and implemented at the level of policy, then the current emphasis on physical 'treatments' would be drastically reduced. It would be replaced by two types of professional activity: the first would be in terms of being listened to and responded to empathically (in other words, the psychological needs of clients would be taken much more seriously than they have been to date); the second would be in terms of the recognition of the centrality of *social* needs. Professional help would facilitate access to the latter. The emphasis would be upon advocating the clients' autonomy and citizenship in society. This is often discussed now in terms of the difference between empowerment and 'treatment' (or 'intervention'). Thus mental health workers would be counsellors and advocates, or 'rights workers'.

As we indicated earlier, the present trend is towards professional preferences for more specialised skills, which means more of the same of what our respondents criticise. As we indicated above, one educational policy implication of this has to do with professional training. If mental health professionals continue to preoccupy themselves with more and more technical mystique, this will favour outcome 1 above, not a more user-friendly service. However, professionals are not a monolithic group, and a different set of values can also be identified amongst certain groups of mental health workers. Many progressive workers are campaigning, like users, for advocacy, self-advocacy and for a new type of mental health policy which is benign and user-centred. For example, the trade unions (which were previously lukewarm or even hostile to community care) have done an about-turn and are supporting community-based alternatives.

One alternative to traditional asymmetrical forms of expert services, where one party is clearly designated as being in the wrong, sick and always inferior, the other designated as correct, well and superior, is that of mutual aid or self-help. A potential basis for such a development can be seen in the organisation of the current self-advocacy movement. The users' movement has shown how one of the most disempowered groups in society is capable of highly effective collective action. Building on this, state agencies could provide the physical setting and support services for self-help groups to exist in each locality. These groups might operate in autonomous voluntary sector projects or in the primary care or local authority sector. These mutual aid projects would emphasise 'ordinary' and equal relationships, as well as giving people with problems access to others who had shared difficulties and could respond empathically.

A re-evaluation of the role of non-medical services under this second alternative outcome would be evident. An increase in the availability of housing, the removal of discrimination in employment practices and a review of social security benefit levels were all implicated in our respondents' views about service provision. Given that recovery from mental health problems is a function of social opportunities, particularly as regards accommodation and employment, policy-makers might place housing and income maintenance at the centre of their thoughts. This is possible for two reasons. The plight of homeless people in general (a large number of whom have been identified as having mental health problems) presents a problem for current welfare policies. Specifically, the 'release' and relocation of patients from hospital to seaside board-and-lodging accommodation, far away from the localities to which patients previously belonged, has become the focus of media and public concern which has required justification by health and local authorities. Thus one of the consequences of de-institutionalisation policies has been to start to redefine a problem hitherto viewed as part and parcel of the 'mental illness' services.

A user-centred policy would thus keep the issue of housing, not illness, as the priority. It is likely that the extent to which housing and other social resources are viewed as a central tenet in the maintenance of mental health will depend on how successfully hospital-based management is promoted as the solution to homeless people with mental health problems. It will also depend on how the relationship between mental distress and homelessness is portrayed. If the latter is seen in terms of homelessness being detrimental to mental health, rather than 'mental illness' giving rise to homelessness, then housing and other social resources will become a central part of policy-making.[11]

This conceivable social model, however, will operate at the expense not only of hospital-based provision but also of sections of the mental health professions, in particular psychiatry. Although there would, amongst other things, still be an obvious need for the counselling/advocacy role outlined above, their present numerical presence would be called into question. The indications are that progressive reforms are favoured when dominant professionals are thin on the ground. For instance, in Italy, where major progressive reforms in mental health have taken place, there are less than one-third of the number of psychiatrists than in the UK.[12]

Indications from our data regarding the negative evaluation of psychiatrists suggests that, if a user-led model starts to assert itself, then it is likely that there would be demands for the role of psychiatrists to change. The emergence of such a de-medicalisation strategy can be seen in recent campaigns around treatment. Campaigning groups, such as Survivors Speak Out, and the appearance of new voluntary groups such as Tranx (which aims to help people come off psychotropic drugs), indicate a challenge to the legitimacy of medical interventions.

Ironically, perhaps, given the criticisms that have been made of the applicability of a bio-medical model in mental health services, it is feasible that demands for a change in the psychiatrist's role would imply the adoption of one more akin to that of a proper physician. Our respondents complained that their physical problems were often not taken seriously, especially those resulting from drug side-effects. It is commonplace for psychiatric patients at present to be given powerful and dangerous drugs on a long term basis with poor or non-existent monitoring.[13] The recurrent exposure of patients to brain and liver damage (as the data on drug treatment indicated) suggests the need for a new role for psychiatrists as more efficient physicians. From our data there does appear to be some support for a limited role for drugs as part of short-term crisis management. In this context, a focus on minimising drug dosages, attention to informed consent and to their responsibilities for protecting recipients of drugs from toxic effects might shape the modified role of psychiatrists.

A reduction in the number of psychiatrists does not imply that an expansion in other professional groups would be desirable or necessary. The whole question we are trying to raise here is that user-centred policy formation is likely to be defined by an improvement in *social and material* opportunities and rights, not necessarily by a change in the ratio of professionals to users. This is not to argue for the abolition of professionals but, if they no longer retain exclusive rights to define what constitutes a good service or policy, other priorities (apart from their own concerns) are likely to emerge. It may be that the model described above implies an emphasis on a different type of worker who focuses on providing practical help and support.

The question of interests

Having rehearsed these two possible outcomes, what interests exist in society which might seek to push for one rather than the other? As far as the first is concerned, three main lobbies can be identified. The first and most obvious of these relates to traditionalists within the psychiatric profession. It is likely that they will continue to argue for the retention of hospital-based psychiatry in order to hang on to their existing powers of medical authority. Beds, both symbolically and practically, provide them with this authority. The DGH units (and even the old 'bins') would preserve this medical privilege.

Close allies of this medical group would be those lobbies in the voluntary sector, like SANE and the NSF, which also favour a medical model, enforced 'treatment' and the physical removal of madness from society. Relatives' interests and those of users inevitably clash at times, and this is reflected in these pressure groups.

The third interest group that is likely to favour the first scenario is the drug industry. Biological psychiatry clearly favours their profits. Those diagnosed as schizophrenic currently are prescribed both major tranquillisers and other drugs to offset their side effects. Our data also showed the extent of polypharmacy within a psychiatric population. The widespread use of drugs in psychiatry is a constant source of profits for the pharmaceutical industry. Their continued funding of psychiatric research is likely to favour and legitimise their central role in mental health, as well as reinforcing the Victorian medical model of mental illness.

It is not only the power of these declared and clearly defined interests which is likely to make this outcome more rather than less likely. More implicitly, so too are certain characteristics of the British social policy-making machinery. The inequitable split in resources between health and social services, as far as mental health provision is concerned, was mentioned earlier. Such measures as joint planning and finance initiatives, designed to overcome this split, have been less than successful. In other words, at a local level, the content and form of mental health services have remained fairly impervious to 'top-down' reforms.

Also, as a recent health policy analysis[14] has suggested, normal health policy planning is characterised by 'decrementalism' (planning which centres around the making of small reductions) or 'incrementalism' (planning centred around small increases in business budgets). This involves speedy decisions being made by a few key people, in a context where the language of crisis predominates. This 'crisis' planning is characterised by expediency and short-term goals being preferred by those directly involved in the planning; this approach therefore undermines or counteracts agreed long-term policy goals. This pragmatic and *ad hoc* health policy-making process is likely to lead to half-baked change, which tends to favour the status quo.

The prevailing interests of the three groups mentioned above, are together powerful forces which favour the first scenario. However, they are faced by another set of interests which favour the second, more progressive, outcome. In government, both political parties have, since the 1970s, signalled their principled agreement to community care. Whether they have pursued this with sufficient intensity is a moot point. Certainly, even those who agree with de-institutionalisation have yet to be convinced that this has led to genuine and acceptable community care. Our data reveals the inertia of the hospital system as one reason behind this problem. Nonetheless, it is unlikely that either political party will support the full-blooded return to the old asylum system.

However, what neither party has done is question vigorously the appropriateness of hospital-based psychiatry and medical treatments. The imbalance of funding highlights this, as does the tendency of both parties to continue to place the Royal College of Psychiatrists at the centre of their policy advice. However, the vigorous pursuit of general management by government during the 1980s, which is set to intensify over the next decade, brings into play the possibility of vociferously questioning clinical effectiveness and efficiency, and an alignment of general managers with non-professional interests.

A recent study by Strong and Robinson[15] identified a strong commitment on the part of general managers to consumerism. They found that general managers perceived themselves as having a central role to play in stimulating professional staff to treat clients as customers rather than patients. Thompson[16] also notes that, in rising to the challenge of 'new managerialism', one strategy entails managers distancing themselves from health care professionals, opting instead to build alternative coalitions. This potential de-stabilisation of medical authority by general management from within the state has been reinforced by a crucial second lobby, which we noted in the first chapter: the growth of the mental health users' movement. Although still a nascent social movement in Britain, its recent organisational capability has begun to have an impact on local and national politicians and managers of statutory services. If organisations like Survivors Speak Out continue to grow in strength, traditional psychiatry will have to manage a new range of threats to its legitimacy and existence. This emphasis on campaigning around self-advocacy, along with the more established advocacy role of MIND, is likely to push harder and harder against the traditional assumptions operating on the content as well as form of services. Campaigns focused on ECT and major tranquillisers will constitute this push, as will demands about citizenship: the right to housing and employment, the right to informed consent, the right to genuine choice, and the right to be treated with respect and dignity. Whatever else hospital run-down has done, it has exposed a number of these contentious political grievances which were previously shut away. To quote a mixed metaphor from Peter Campbell, the secretary of Survivors Speak Out, 'The cat is out of the bag and amongst the pigeons.'

The direction in which these campaigns from below develop will be all-important. It is quite understandable that many of the individual and collective grievances which psychiatric patients articulate are about their disaffection with their treatment at the hands of professionals. However, this also has the consequence of tying users' campaigning to the 'enemy' of psychiatric professionals, which may deflect energy and attention from wider social considerations. It is likely that the success of the users' movement in moving towards the second outcome will, to a significant extent, depend on the ability to broaden its campaigning beyond the important but narrow agenda of seeking improved professional services.

The growth, since the mid-1980s, of the importance within radical political culture of different interests which are removed from traditional class interests (race, gender, age, disability, and so on) are also likely to provide an environment which is receptive to demands from previously marginalised groups, such as mental health users. Such an environment is likely to be reinforced by other radical community health groups (for example, the Disability Alliance or women's health groups), which have singled out dominant health care practices as an intrinsic part of their difficulties. The variable and decentralised nature of this form of political culture may make the extent of the success of the second outcome a local or regional matter.

A final but crucial consideration about the future of British mental health provision is the likely prospects there are for the genuine de-marginalisation of mental health users. This is complicated and begs certain questions, such as what forces in society might encourage a more tolerant and fair appreciation of people who act in a distressed and often unintelligible way? At the moment, prospects for the de-marginalisation of those labelled as neurotic seem hopeful in that they induce a common sympathy. An example of this was the public and media support for the minor tranquilliser campaign in the mid-1980s.[17]

By contrast, the media images of those labelled as psychotic seem to work against their interests.[18] They are generally depicted as dangerous and sinister, they have become the 'other'. An exemplar of this can be identified in a recent SANE poster campaign emphasising such slogans as 'He thinks he's Jesus. You think he's a killer. They think he's fine.' It seems, then, that the broad conceptual discrepancy between those people variously described as 'mad' or 'psychotic' and those described as 'neurotic' or the 'worried well', arouse different feelings and political responses. The former are still seen as alien and threatening; the latter are seen as distressed and deserving of sympathy and support. So when the question of citizenship is considered for users of services, the former group look likely to continue to be treated prejudicially, whilst the latter group maybe treated more favourably.

How can we account for this discrepancy? It would seem that the former group are guilty of transgressing social norms in an unpredictable way. This unpredictability is at the heart of the unsympathetic and prejudicial response they frequently meet in others. Recently, Jonathan Miller summarised this predicament as follows:

It appears in the family first of all and then of course it appears in public places. There's a vast, very complicated, unwritten constitution of conduct which allows us to move with confidence through public spaces, and we can instantly and by a very subtle process recognise someone who is breaking that constitution. They're talking to themselves; they're not moving at the same rate; they're moving at different angles; they're not avoiding other people with the skill that

pedestrians do in the street. The speed with which normal users of
public places can recognise someone else as not being a normal user of
it is where madness appears.[19]

Whilst we think this is a fair summary of what constitutes
madness, what Miller goes on to prescribe is at the heart of the
issue about citizenship and people with mental health problems.
He says: 'there *has* to be some sort of unwritten constitution,
which allows us to move with fluency from one place to another
without having to test the water step by step' (our emphasis).
However, this general prescription does not, of course, tell us how
flexible such a constitution should or could be. People are only
self-evidently mad in relation to specific cultural norms. These
norms can vary over time and place and can be re-negotiated. The
question, then, is whether this constitution could or should be
made more tolerant of people who are different than has often
been the case.

This tolerance of difference itself can only be built upon a more
fair and accurate acknowledgement of the reality of mad
behaviour. For example, the emphasis in the media on
dangerousness is actually unwarranted. The overwhelming
majority of people who break the rules to which Miller draws
our attention are perplexing, but they are harmless and docile and
do not constitute a *real* threat to anyone around them. However,
the unpredictability of those deemed to break social expectations,
without an intelligible reason, then fuels fantasies of threat in
others. Thus, in addition to changes in policy, professional
interventions, treatments and social and material resources, the
extent to which negative representations of psychiatric patients
are overcome will, ultimately, determine the extent of the de-
marginalisation of mental health users in society.

Conclusion

In terms of the two different outcomes we mapped out above for
social policy, the mental health users' movement and its
professional allies will have their work cut out on two fronts.
They will need to persuade government that users' needs are best
framed broadly in personal and social rather than medical terms,
and they will also have to convince the wider public that people
with mental health problems have a right to ask for peaceful co-
existence in society.

Notes and References

1. Stacey, M., *The Sociology of Health and Healing* (London: Unwin Hyman, 1988).
2. Clare, A., *Psychiatry in Dissent* (London: Tavistock, 1979).
3. Blaxter, M., and Paterson, E., *Mother and Daughters: A Three Generational Study of Health Attitudes and Behaviour* (London: Heinemann Educational, 1982).
4. Cornwell, J., *Hard-Earned Lives* (London: Tavistock, 1984); Thorogood, N., 'Afro-Caribbean women's experience of the health services', *New Community*, 15, 3, pp. 335–41.
5. Stimson, G., and Webb, B., *Going to See the Doctor:The Consultation Process in General Practice* (London: Routledge & Kegan Paul, 1975).
6. Parsons, T., *The Social System* (London: Routledge & Kegan Paul, 1951), ch. 10.
7. Cornwell, J., *Hard-Earned Lives*.
8. These would give psychiatrists the right to force medication on people refusing to 'comply' with treatment whilst living in the community.
9. Goodwin, S., *Community Care and the Future of Mental Health Service Provision* (Aldershot: Avebury, 1990).
10. Sayce, L., *Waiting for Community Care* (London: MIND, 1990).
11. Although the success of this might depend as much on the response by housing departments as it does on mental health policy-makers.
12. World Health Organisation figures, 1985, cited in Sartorius, N., 'Mental Health Care in Continental Europe', in Marks, I. and Scott, R. *Mental Health Care Delivery*.
13. Russel-Davies, D. 'Toxic Psychiatry', *Open Mind*, 55, 9 (1990).
14. Small, N., *Politics and Planning in the National Health Service* (Milton Keynes: Open University Press, 1989).
15. Strong, P. and Robinson, J., *The NHS Under New Management* (Milton Keynes: Open University Press, 1990).
16. Thompson, D., 'Coalitions and Conflict in the National Health Service: Some Implications for General Management' *Sociology of Health and Illness*, 9, 2, pp. 127–53
17. Gabe, J. and Bury, M., 'Tranquillisers as a Social Problem', *The Sociological Review*, 36, 2 pp. 320–52
18. Adlam, D., 'TV Crazy', unpublished MSc dissertation, London School of Economics, 1987.
19. Miller, J., 'The Doctor's Dilemma: Miller on Madness', *Open MIND*, 49 (Feb/March, 1991) p. 31.

Methodological Appendix

Our intention at the outset of the People First project was to utilise both quantitative and qualitative methods in order to reveal and understand the overall view patients have of mental health facilities. In so doing, we were conscious of the shortcomings of previous research which had taken either a purely qualitative or a purely quantitative approach.

Two main methodological weaknesses have been associated with qualitative investigations.[1] First, by concentrating on the effect of mental hospitalisation on the patients, they have tended to exclude the wider views that patients had about their difficulties and their lives. Second, unstructured interviewing techniques fail to explore, in a systematic way, people's attitudes, focusing instead on only on what was mentioned spontaneously in each separate case. This casts doubt on the representativeness of case studies of this type (although it does not invalidate their utility for other purposes). Quantitative studies have suffered from a different weakness. Pre-worded questions in survey research have had a tendency to self-select those who agree with the view advocated in the questions.

The findings of these two methodological approaches have also tended to contradict each other in studies of mental health services. Whereas quantitative research has tended to produce a favourable picture of mental hospitalisation, qualitative studies have depicted psychiatry as being overwhelmingly restrictive and authoritarian. This could be because each of the approaches has tapped different things. Whereas a qualitative approach has concentrated on people's *experiences*, quantitative studies have tried to measure people's *attitudes*. An either/or approach to research methodology has been replaced by a both/and approach in our study, as we view qualitative and quantitative methods as being complimentary rather than antagonistic. This combined approach, we believe, is likely to produce a more sensitive and coherent view of mental patienthood.

Procedure

No fewer than 1000 interview schedules were distributed from the headquarters of National MIND. The sample of users came from two sources. In the main, schedules were sent out to regional offices throughout England and Wales, who distributed them to local MIND associations in their areas. There were no fixed quotas as to how many were to be filled in by each association. This was left to the discretion of the regions, as it was recognised that the differing size, organisation and interest of local groups, and thus their ability to complete interviews, would be variable. A smaller number of schedules were distributed to 'non-MIND' contacts. This included mental health workers in the statutory sector (mainly social services) voluntary organisations and other 'interested' individuals, some of whom were higher education students with an interest in mental health who carried out interviews with people who had previously been admitted to hospital.

The sample

There are few existing criteria of methodological adequacy in relation to the sampling frames for users' views of mental health services. First, there are definitional problems: who constitutes a 'user' of psychiatric services? A wide definition might incorporate, at one extreme, a person going to see a GP for a one-off prescription for minor tranquillisers or a pupil seen once by a mental health professional at a child guidance clinic. At the other extreme, it could include someone held indefinitely under the Mental Health Act as a mentally disordered offender. Though these people may or may not accept the label of psychiatric patient, their experiences, needs, and perceptions would clearly have a limited meaning if they were analysed as a homogeneous group.

In this research we were particularly anxious to avoid accusations that the views of people were not representative of those who are really 'mentally ill'. We also wanted to include those people in a position to have had fairly extensive contact with mental health services. With this in mind, a stipulation for inclusion in the sample was that the person being interviewed was required to have had at least one period of treatment as a psychiatric in-patient. Where organisations had comprehensive lists of people known to fulfil this criterion, it was requested that this be used as the sampling frame and a sample selected at random. In practice, such randomisation occurred rarely, mainly because such administrative records did not exist, but also because methodological pragmatism dictated that the sample and interviewers were volunteers. The amount of time and effort being asked of the interviewers was already substantial, and so the researchers could not impose unreasonable conditions on them. Implicitly, there was a further criterion for selection: in agreeing to participate, respondents defined themselves as users of services.

Another question we addressed was the number of people we should include to obtain a representative sample. The main methodological problem here was choosing an appropriate comparison population. There are no reliable estimates of the number of ex-users in the population. Although the figure of one person in four is often quoted as the number of people who are likely to experience mental health problems during their lifetime, the source of this information is by no means clear. Certainly, compared to the numbers of in-patients admitted to psychiatric hospitals each year, 516 people is an adequate number to meet the normal criteria of representativeness. However, only 37 per cent ($N = 193$) of the sample had been in hospital during the previous 12 months prior to interview, and we also wished to include those who had been in hospital at some time in their psychiatric career. We were concerned to include views about the whole *range* of mental health services and to build a picture of people's perceptions that had emerged over time, rather than merely providing a 'snapshot' of views about their last admission. Thus we did not want to limit the study to those who had been admitted recently. What can be said with certainty in terms of statistical adequacy is that, to date, there is no other study (that we are aware of) which has used anything nearing the numbers used in this survey.

In selecting a sample for a social survey, where the sample is drawn from is as important as adequate numbers. It was mentioned above that two sources were used. Respondents from MIND local associations made up 68 per cent of the total sample: the remaining 32 per cent drawn from other sources. We are aware that one of the criticisms that could be made about the representativeness of the sample is that the MIND respondents might be a predominantly self-selected group who may be more critical about services than other ex-patients. In order to see whether this was the case we compared the responses of the MIND users with the non-MIND respondents and found that there were no statistically significant differences between the two groups.[2]

One of the criticisms that can be made of some health and social services consumer research is that views of users are elicited by professionals on hospital or other service delivery premises. This introduces the tendency towards 'yeah saying' and a bias in favour of high satisfaction rates. Users being investigated by professionals, who are also their clinicians, are clearly likely to be constrained in their critical responses. This may be accentuated in psychiatric patients who stand in a particularly powerless relationship to the health and social services, as they run the risk of losing their liberty through compulsory detention. In this context, the interviewing of users by non-mental health professionals, on non-statutory service territory, is likely to have produced more valid responses than hospital-based research conducted by NHS employees. However, in our study there is the converse danger: a possible over-reporting of positive views about mental health voluntary organisations (particularly MIND). This is particularly relevant to questions in the interview on residential services and the voluntary sector. Although, as mentioned above, cross-checking the views of the MIND sample with the non-MIND group did not reveal any statistically significant differences in terms of views of services, professionals or (as treatment, judged by the extent of qualitiative comments) the MIND respondents appeared to have more to say about their experiences of voluntary organisation services. Additionally, in order to prevent mindless ticking, or 'yeah saying', open-ended questions were designed to compare and contrast views about statutory and voluntary services. This required respondents to elaborate on the *reasons* for their views rather than only using the cruder measure of pre-coded satisfaction rates.

It will be evident from Table A.1 that, in terms of the geographical spread and population concentration, there was a bias towards Wales, the South-East and the North-East of England. This contrasts with the mainstream of mental health research which typically concentrates on the London area (reflecting the hierarchical nature of teaching hospital and resourcing of services). Other areas are often neglected. However, the different geographical bias in our sample (away from London) led to an under-representation of black people in the sample compared to their numbers in the psychiatric system. Though attempts were made to include greater numbers of black people, by approaching organisations with access to black users, only 18 out of the 516 of respondents were of Asian or Afro-Caribbean origin. The slightly higher percentage of women (51 per cent compared to 49 per cent of men) corresponds with the greater proportion of women using in-patient services, although this percentage is still a slight under-representation of women's overall use of services.

Table A1   Regional distribution of sample

Area	%
South-West England	7.7
South-East England	22.9
Greater London	9.7
East Midlands	3.1
West Midlands	6.0
North-East England	9.9
North-West England	7.2
Wales	17.6
Other	15.9

Interviews

The interviews were piloted in Liverpool by two of the authors (Anne Rogers and David Pilgrim) during the summer of 1989. Data collection took place between November 1989 and February 1990. There were 241 questions in all, 38 of which were open-ended. Piloting indicated that completing the schedule took between 2 and 3 hours (indicating the extensive views elicited from each respondent compared to most 'market research' type studies). The length of the schedule, together with the fact that many of the questions were open-ended and required a dialogue to elicit full and rich data, precluded the use of self-administered questionnaires. The interviews were carried out by volunteers in local MIND associations and other organisations. No formal training was given to individual interviewers, although a number of briefing sessions with regional MIND groups were held. Detailed briefing notes on selection, interviewing and probing were included with each schedule. The schedule was divided up into 12 sections which covered the following: circumstance and experience of first mental health problem; treatment from and relations with GPs; psychiatric treatment as a hospital in- and out-patient; experiences of day facilities; OT and IT; rehabilitation and resettlement; residential services in the community; treatment including psychotropic drugs, ECT and psychological therapies; welfare benefits, and the financial and social background of the respondents.

Some pragmatic and ethical dilemmas arose for the interviewers in this study. Two in particular are worth noting here. First, there was a problem in sustaining the momentum of the interview. Thus the last sections on psychological therapies, welfare benefits and background information about the respondents contained more 'missing' responses than the earlier sections on admission to hospital and first mental health problems.

Second, a problem (which led to some abandoned interviews) was that, in recalling their experiences, some respondents became upset. This put the interviewers in a difficult position: should they deal with the distress of the person there and then, and if so, how; should they refer on to another agency; and was it legitimate to carry out this form of research at all? We received a number of letters from interviewers complaining about the distress caused to them and respondents. During our piloting, we were aware of the possible distress which might ensue, for some, from a detailed recollection of painful memories, but we rejected the idea of discontinuing or modifying the research. There was an obvious interest in wanting to continue the research project we had started but, additionally, the researchers felt that it would be more irresponsible to abandon or modify the project for these reasons because we would be showing undue paternalism (similar to many of the complaints of services expressed by users) by preventing the full force of emotions being expressed about this area of people's lives. The complaints of some of the interviewers also brought home the extent to which it is the feelings invoked in others (that is, not the patients themselves) which often governs or informs decision-making in conditions of uncertainty about mental distress.

There were some advantages to using untrained interviewers. The quality of the responses suggested that, generally, a good rapport had been established between interviewer and interviewee conducive to disclosure. This may not have happened to the same extent had the person been an anonymous interviewer who had had little contact with service-users. The overall richness of data obtained, and the visible careful note taking on the overwhelming majority of the returned schedules, sheds some doubt on advice given in methods textbooks. Such books tend to emphasise the need for extensive training of interviewers in social research.

Inevitably issues arose which were related to the reliability and validity of the data. The lack of information given to patients was, not surprisingly, sometimes reflected in some response inaccuracies, for instance in the reporting of the categories of drugs people had been prescribed. Respondents were asked to recall the type of drugs that they had been prescribed (such as anti-depressants) and the *names* of their drugs. Because of the researchers' knowledge of psychiatric medication, they sometimes noted a mismatch in the two listings by some respondents. When this occurred, the responses were recoded as missing values.

It was also recognised, with the benefit of hindsight, that there were some omissions in the questionnaire schedule. There was a failure to include a global rating for in-patient services. (This was not an omission for other parts of the service.) To compensate for this oversight, comparisons were made on the basis of judgements from results about *specific* aspects of the services (aspects of hospital staff behaviour towards patient's for example) and by counting negative and positive responses to open-ended questions about the respondents' experience of hospitalisation. In this way an aggregate global response was deduced.

With regard to the qualitative responses, it was interesting to note that the continuum between 'public ' and 'private' accounts given about health services noted by other researchers[3] was rarely in evidence in users' accounts in this study. ('Public' accounts refer to the tendency on the part of respondents to give a 'public relations' version of reality – for example, 'nurses and doctors did their best in the circumstances' – whilst in-depth interviewing usually reveals 'private' accounts which might include a hidden amount of dissatisfaction and criticism).

The departure of our data from the pattern reported by Cornwell and Thorogood (in relation to their sample of 'physical' rather than mental patients) may have been for two reasons. The one-to-one interviews were not as open-ended as in these other studies (that is, the questions were more focused on eliciting people's views about particular elements of service provision, so there was no need to couch responses in an 'acceptable' manner). Alternatively, and/or additionally, the split of public/private accounts usually suggests some ambivalence about the positive and negative benefits received from health services. It may have been that, with users of mental health services, dissatisfaction was so marked that the public accounts were often dispensed with.

Analysis of data

The 240 fixed choice questions were analysed using the Statistical Package for the Social Sciences. At various points in the book, data about particular sub-groups have been used rather than the whole sample population (such as women, or those who have been in hospital for more than one year). To an extent the quantitative material also guided the analysis of the wide-ranging qualitative data obtained. For example, it was possible to select out those cases which had made positive or negative ratings about a particular aspect of service provision and then to go back and examine in further detail the reasons why people were dissatisfied or satisfied. At other times, open-ended questions were analysed in their entirety, or themes were identified and expanded on in the analysis and presentation of data. Throughout, exemplars of *typical* responses have been given to illuminate how users perceive contemporary British mental health services. This book has presented a comprehensive, though not total, list of the findings in the wake of the data analysis.

Notes and References

1. Bryman, A., *Quantity and Quality in Social Research* (London: Unwin Hyman, 1988), pp. 161.
2. Using Chi-Square significance tests.
3. Cornwell, J., *Hard Earned Lives: Accounts of Health and Illness from East London* (London: Tavistock, 1984); Thorogood, N., 'Afro-Caribbean Women's Accounts of the NHS', *New Community*, 15, 3, pp. 335–41.

Name Index

Subject Index